A Slow Slide into Nothing

Rosemary Christle-Renaud

Suzanne,

Thank you for your support of reading my book. And, all of yours lovely comments when I would run into you. Here is to our book club.

Rosemary 2015

This book is dedicated to my Mother, Ruthanna (Corki) Keffaber Christle, who was a great teacher to me, and so many others. It is also dedicated to my sister Rocky, who has been my traveling companion down many roads from childhood to college, young women to new mothers, to empty-nesters. She has been my confidante' and guide. She is my sister and always my friend.

What began as a series of essays, written over the course of some very emotional, trying years gradually transformed itself into this book. The words I have written are my own based upon my recollection of events and my feelings at the time. This book was not written with the intention to hurt feelings but rather, as a way for me to allow my emotions to fall across a page in written word and therefore escape from the confines of my stressed and weary mind.

I have always believed that family dynamics can be difficult. Birth order, sibling rivalry and personality can make getting along problematic. These traits, mingled with the emotion of watching one's mother slowly die, can cause words and actions that in better times most likely would not have surfaced.

Therefore, I also dedicate this book to the family that Joe and Corki Christle raised: all of us.

Our Family home in Wabash, Indiana
August 2000

When I stepped onto the porch I expected to see Mom at the door. Instead, I had to let myself in. There she sat in the dark living room. I glanced around remembering the many family pictures taken in front of the salmon pink limestone fireplace which filled the wall at the far end of the living room. I looked for the family portraits and my wedding picture. I waited for the years of childhood memories to come flooding back but they did not, could not, as I looked at my mother. She looked frail, tired and scared. Her clothing was dirty and covered with stains. I was taken aback. *How had my mother let herself get to this state?* Mom always took pride in her appearance. She had dressed competently as a high school counselor, later professionally as the city court judge. Now she wore clothing that did not match. Food had dribbled down the front of her shirt. Seeing her this way terrified me. I took a deep breath; I struggled not to appear shocked. Mom seemed embarrassed by the way she was dressed and the mess the house was in. I quivered with the gradual realization she was no longer capable of performing these daily tasks.

Mom had already begun her slow slide into nothing...

## Prologue


In the spring of 2007, my widowed mother came to live with me in my upstate New York home. She left behind all that she knew and had acquired from a lifetime spent living in Central Indiana. It had been apparent for some time to my siblings and me, that Mom was struggling to live on her own, but my mother's independent streak and her fierce Irish-German stubbornness did not allow her to leave her residence of fifty years easily.

When Mom moved in with my family and me, I believed she was still grieving the death of my father, her husband of fifty-five years. Through concerned hometown friends and relatives, I learned Mom no longer participated in the activities she once enjoyed; she now rarely ventured out of her home. All signs of depression, I assumed. Naively, I imagined that once Mom came to live with me she would find a new direction in life from the love my family would give her. I hoped that my relationship with Mom would evolve into the nurturing mother-daughter connection I had sought for years. Yet, after only a few short weeks, it became quite apparent all of my assumptions were completely wrong.

My mother's dementia was not the ending I had in mind for our story together. Eventually, during the six years that she lived with or near me, we did develop a new relationship; a bond I had not considered but one still based on trust and love. Getting to that final rapport took years of struggle between us. In the beginning of our journey, even though Mom could hardly manage to care for herself, we struggled to establish who was in charge. Mom understood she was the parent and thus felt she should be in control. She resented being told what to do by one of her children. I, on the other hand, waffled between years of being the respectful child and now having to take the lead. At each stage of Mom's dementia, new battle lines were drawn and settled until finally, after several years, her confidence in me was ascertained. That hard won trust was required for a loving bond to blossom into total faith and for Mom to realize that decisions made on her behalf were always for the best.

My emotional journey also sparked a transition of my faith. My feelings about established religion had been evolving for several years. Soon after Mom moved in with me, I stopped my already rare attendance at Mass. My choice had nothing to do with my mother. Rather, it was a decision that had been growing within me. I felt more in touch with my idea of God when I was out in nature or doing an activity with my friends or family. Mass became a ritual that I dreaded and, consequently, attained nothing from. The further I became involved with Mom's care, the more I became aware of an inner voice guiding me. I am, by character, a non-confrontational person. Still, as I heard myself boldly questioning doctors, working with insurance companies, dealing with family members and lawyers, I discovered the words coming from my lips sometimes were not my own. I had not thought to say these words, yet there they were being said. When I mentioned these events to my sister, Rhonda, she opened my eyes to the spiritual guidance of Angels. She taught me these beings are with us constantly and can lead us with inner voices or other outward signs. Because of what I had experienced, I concluded Rhonda was correct. I began to follow my intuition, or Angels. In doing so, I felt more at peace and stopped second-guessing myself. My spirituality grew and I connected with these higher beings that were sent to guide and comfort me. It was my Angels, I believe, who first directed me to begin writing.

I did not write my thoughts down immediately upon my mother's arrival. After many months of growing frustrations, I realized I needed an avenue to release the anxiety growing within me. I recalled earlier in my life the joy I felt when writing. Listening to guidance from my Angels, I felt driven to return to the art of journaling. I joined a writing group at a local bookstore and during my first session, I met a group of novice writers. We formed a lasting bond that strengthened as we each transformed into authors. It was this group and our instructor that gave me the courage to record my feelings. Even so, I did not believe I would take my thoughts and turn them into this book. As my writing developed, I realized my required weekly class essays could be a comfort to others, those walking zombie-like through days of endless dementia care, making difficult life-altering decisions, as I was. Consequently, I continued in my pursuit of finishing this book not only for myself, but also for others who will travel down the path my mother had taken me. I hope it will bring caregivers comfort and the knowledge they are not alone in their struggles.

To do justice to my mother I have given you, the reader, a brief history of Mom's life. I felt that was important so that you, too, can understand the sorrow I felt watching this woman, who accomplished so much in her eighty-five years, slide into nothing.

The essays written about the journey Mom and I took together fall in chronological order. It is my hope that you, the reader, will garner a sense of camaraderie from my honest account, which includes periods of personal pain, incredible grief, love and, believe it or not, moments of therapeutic laughter.

This book is for all of us struggling together in what I call "The Caretaker Nation."

Table of Contents

The Early Years

My mother was what some would call a free spirit. Others would call her wild. From stories I remember Mom telling me and from listening to her conversations with siblings and friends over many years, I thought I knew my mother. It wasn't until I was cleaning out my childhood home and found her girlhood diary that I gained far more knowledge about the person whom I call Mom.

Ruthanna Keffaber was born on July 7, 1924. Ruthanna, commonly known as Corki, a nickname she somehow picked up in her childhood, had two older brothers and was the middle of three sisters. Intelligent, she graduated from college the first time with a teacher's certificate. Much later, she would receive a Master's degree in counseling and would have completed her PhD except she chose not to write her final dissertation. She was a singer with a band, wife, mother of seven, teacher, counselor and city court judge. Mom was also a voracious reader. She loved politics and she played a mean game of Bridge. For that matter, she was merciless at most games.

Mom grew up in a massive three-story farmhouse once owned by family members of the turn-of-the-century novelist and amateur naturalist, Gene Stratton Porter. Typical for the time the house did not have electricity or running water, but some rooms were lighted with Argon gas. Her family home, located in Wabash County, was near the city of Wabash, the first electrically lighted city in the world thanks to four Brush lights placed on top of the county courthouse. Mom was witness to this unique experience from her distant farmhouse as those infamous lights shone across the flat Indiana prairie.

My maternal grandmother, Marie Hippensteel Keffaber, was of Irish and German descent; she had an Irish complexion with beautiful auburn hair. My grandfather, Harry Valentine Keffaber, was one generation removed from Germany and, with his piercing good looks, towered over Marie.

Mom did not recall much about her paternal grandfather, who emigrated from Germany when he was a young boy of six, but she did remember him in this way:

Pop's father was very mean spirited. He often spoke about us children in German, but we could tell he was not giving us compliments. When he got older and couldn't walk, he would try to trip me with his crutch as I walked by his chair. I learned to take a wide path around him. And, I was his favorite.

Mom's parents married young. Marie was only sixteen and Harry was twenty-one. Mom always gave this account of her parent's marriage at such an early age:

Pop and my mother went out on a date in the buggy and fell asleep. The horse, feeling the loose reins, wandered home to the barn and his feed. Pop and Mother woke to find my grandfather standing on the porch with a bullwhip. I often thought that was when they had to get married.

My grandparents were a happy couple and settled quickly onto a farm of their own. It was here that Mom and her siblings Paul, Otis, Betty and Maxine grew up. Both my grandparents were members of the Christian Science religion. One small part of that faith is that people have the ability to heal themselves of all illnesses through prayer and belief in Jesus. This belief tragically led to my grandmother's premature death, an event that haunted Mom most of her life.

When Mom was five years old, her mother became ill with appendicitis, but remaining a true Christian Scientist she refused to go to the hospital. She died several days later when her appendix ruptured. My grandmother's death at such a young age, while still in her twenties, was a tragedy felt by all members of the extended family. From comments Mom made over the years it appears that this incident led to arguments between the two families. Marie's family believed Harry should have forced her to seek medical care; Harry's family believed he did what Marie wanted. Through the turmoil, with no one taking the time to explain what happened to her mother, Mom was left to grieve on her own. In the common tradition of that era, Marie was laid out before burial in the family parlor.

"One night I snuck downstairs and touched my mother. I was alarmed because she was so cold. That always stayed with me," Mom recalled.

Mom remembered her mother as warm, a cuddler and fun loving. "She wore her shoes on the wrong feet just to make us children laugh."

Suddenly, without explanation, Mom's beloved mother was gone. This led to an episode at the funeral that Mom grieved about the rest of her life. There were times when she would become melancholy. During one of these periods, she spoke of her sorrow:

> At the funeral, I was very young and frightened. I did not really understand what was going on and no one bothered to explain it to me. When they came to take my mother's body out of the house, I would not let go of her hand. My father, in a moment of frustration, promised he would

buy me new overalls if I behaved. I agreed,
but immediately regretted my choice as I
watched them carry my mother out the
door.

Marie's family reached out to her five children, which
gave Mom the opportunity to be surrounded in her
formative years by her maternal extended family. At one
point in her life, Mom stayed with her grandmother during
the day to assist her. Mom remembered laughter was a
large part of their relationship. With a twinkle in her eye,
Mom would relate:

My grandmother and I were old buddies.
Once, while we planted the vegetable
garden, she was overcome with giggles and
fell to the ground. Grandmother was very
short and heavy. She struggled, but couldn't
get up. As a young girl, I was too small to
help her regain her footing so I ran down
the lane to where my uncles were working
in the field. Alarmed that something terrible
had happened, they dashed back to the

house and were stunned to find their mother laying in the yard laughing. My uncles loved that I was so good to their mother. They gave me gifts all the time like white rabbits with pink eyes.

Mom's Uncle Willis lived across the street. Mom remembered that one day her grandmother called her in from playing with her cousins so she could deliver a hot toddy to Uncle Willis who was very ill. Mom assumed it was some sort of alcohol mixed with brewed tea.

Her grandmother explained, "Now, you take this hot toddy over to Uncle Willis and read to him."

"So I did. I could hear the other kids playing as I read for hours, until he passed away."

Sometimes Mom got to visit her uncles and their families who had left farming and moved into the town of Wabash, a community that thrived from the westward movement of the Erie Canal. The visits were full of excitement and new experiences for a girl who lived out on a farm. One uncle owned a filling station, a new concept at the time.

"I loved going to visit my aunts and uncles. They lived in Wabash and their houses had running water and electricity."

Fortunately, for Mom and her siblings, Harry's family also remained very close to the children. Mom and her sister Maxine, who was only nine months old when their mother passed away, often stayed with one of Harry's brothers or sisters and their families. Uncle Herman and his wife, who had no children of their own, grew very fond of Mom and, out of love and concern, proposed adoption.

"Uncle Herman and his wife wanted to adopt me. Pop asked if I wanted to live with them, but I cried, 'Oh no, Pop, I want to stay with my brothers and sisters.'"

Later in life reflecting on that decision, Mom always said with a slight chuckle, "Maybe I should have moved in with Uncle Herman, he and his wife had no children and they left a lot of money behind when they died."

Even though Harry had the help of his extended family it was difficult for him to care for his five children, but he somehow managed that while running his farm. As Mom matured in age there were times when she was allowed to stay home with her father:

> Pop was afraid to leave me alone because
> I was so young. So I followed him
> everywhere. If he was shucking corn, I was
> there. If he was in the fields, I was with him.
> I think that is why I was always his favorite.

Mom wasn't the only one helping her father. Life on a working farm was hard, physical work. There was always something to be done and many times the whole family had to help out. Mom more than once lamented, "I was never trained to do anything except hard work.

However, that was not all true. Mom also talked many times about extended family dinners and the fun the cousins had together:

> Everyone went to Grandma's house on
> Sunday. We played with our cousins. We all
> wanted to go to Grandma's house. On the
> Fourth of July, they just handed us
> fireworks and we blew our fingertips off. No

one bothered to watch us. We would play "Becum," a game of hide-and-seek combined with tag. My brother Paul always climbed to the highest spot on the house. That way he could wave people free, but never get caught. We always knew to look for him up there, but could never see him unless he wanted us to.

Sometimes my grandfather would entice his children to finish their farm work with the promise of fun. Occasionally, that meant a visit to the town of Lagro. A village established by Irish immigrants on the Wabash and Erie Canal. The dream of growing the area into a bustling city never materialized and died with the dismantling of the canal system. Yet, these immigrants lovingly built a small Catholic Church, Saint Patrick's, which is where my Mom one day would joyfully witness me marrying my husband, Paul Renaud.

The visits to the small town on hot summer nights often included free movies shown on a cotton sheet that was strung across the local thoroughfare. People bustled in from all over the county for these big nights. Friends, young and old, got a chance to catch up with each other. Mom looked forward to seeing many of her gang, as she called them, on those evenings.

"Pop would say, 'If you get all your potatoes done, we'll go to the movies.' We always had to get a job done. In town the parents would sit together, but the gang always sat on the wall."

Along with the occasional movie in town, Mom found entertainment in playing the piano, a skill she learned from her Uncle Herman.

"Uncle Herman would play a note on his tuba and then I would find it on the piano as we sat together in his quiet parlor. He would say, 'Now, that is an A'– that's how I learned to play the piano."

Herman and my grandfather played in a local band. With Herman on the tuba, Harry chose the percussion route, apparently because he believed girls liked drummers. My mother often spoke of her beloved Uncle Herman and admired his venturous spirit citing his annual trips to the

Indianapolis 500 for most of his adult life. Once there, he joined fellow musicians in a band formed for the occasion. It was an all day celebration. Mom explained this event many times to her children as we prepared for our own race day festivities:

> Uncle Hermann would leave very early in the morning and drive to Indianapolis. He played with the band before the race and also performed the National Anthem. Then he would stay and watch the race, getting home very late, and way after dark. Because you know back then, the racecars only went fifty to sixty miles per hour. The race would take all day.

Harry would have liked to attend the Indy 500 with his brother, but he had a young family to worry about and no mother to care for them. In desperation to keep his household together, Harry hired several housekeepers, many of whom robbed the family and, one-by-one, left in the middle of the night, according to Mom. Eventually, he hired a woman named Daisy. She was a widow with grown children. A relationship evolved between the two adults; Mom always felt their bond was one of respect rather than true love. When Mom was in elementary school, Daisy and Harry married and took a short trip to the World's Fair in Chicago for their honeymoon.

The relationship between Daisy and the older children was not an easy one. Mom expressed many times that she felt Daisy was mean and unfair. Mom often said, "Daisy had favorites and I was not one of them. She made us all share the same tub water and washcloth. Usually, I was last in the tub and by then the water was cold and dirty."

Mom, perhaps because of her disagreements with Daisy or because she had become accustomed to them, often spent her days out in the fields riding on her Pop's lap while he plowed. Years later, Mom relented on her feelings somewhat. "Our house was always kept as a shrine to our mother, Marie. How awful it must have been for Daisy."

Harry and Marie Keffaber,
my grandparents
circa 1920

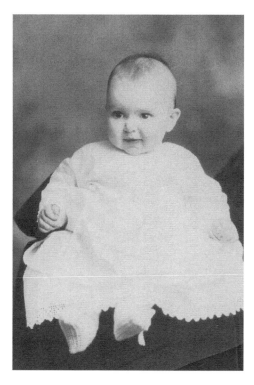

Mom as an infant
1924

Odie, Mom, Paul, Betty
circa 1926

Mom, age 5
1929

**The Teen Years**

As Mom got older, she helped her father by taking over more of the work in the fields and driving the tractor herself. This served many purposes. Alone amid the corn, risking punishment from her father, she wore a daring tube top to get a suntan, very risqué for the times. I always believed this was a precursor to her adventurous escapades before she met her future husband. (Perhaps Uncle Herman had more influence than he ever imagined.) Staying outside also kept Mom from dealing with Daisy's daily badgering.

On the farm was a big creek and Mom remembered many lazy afternoons spent fishing there, listening to the buzz of the insects hovering around her in the Midwestern summer humidity. If she wasn't running through the fields with her brother Odie and his friends, Mom could be found in their front yard cradled in the branches of her favorite tree where she would sit for hours reading, letting herself be rocked while enjoying the cool breeze. It was also a great place to hide from her younger sister, Maxine, whom Mom found annoying with her requests for her older sister to come play.

On rare occasions, Mom was allowed to make the mile trek to the corner store with her girlfriends to buy candy. They passed by a neighbor's house that often flew a communist flag which as my mother always said was an odd political statement for that era.

There were several instances when Mom remembered swimming with friends and her older brothers in one of the farm ponds scattered amongst the corn, beans and wheat:

> One time while swimming in a pond, several boys began to tease me. They kept pushing me under and became so involved with their game they did not notice I couldn't catch my breath. It was terrifying. I struggled to come up for air, only to be pushed down under the water again. I became panic-stricken and almost drowned.

Mom did not enjoy swimming after that and she made it a priority for her children to participate in swim lessons until we all became excellent swimmers. As she explained to us over the years, "I knew I would never be able to jump into the water and save you if something happened."

Along with her anxiety over water, Mom often related to us why she had an irrational fear of snakes:

> Once, while my friends and I were driving our buggy on a small country lane, we came upon a brown paper bag. The bag was moving so we pulled over, thinking it was a small animal trapped inside. As my friend opened the bag, with horror we discovered several snakes coiled within. The snakes hissed and struck at us as they began slithering out.

Mom loved to play practical jokes. Getting into trouble, either from Daisy or her Pop, did not seem to stop her from creating mischief. She loved both of her brothers, but Odie was Mom's favorite probably because they were closer in age. She often told this tale as one of her favorite childhood memories:

>Odie was afraid of the dark, but it was his job to blow out the lantern at the top of the stairs before going to bed. He would then run the length of the hall and hurl himself into the safety of his blankets. One night Maxine and I moved Odie's bed. As usual, he came running down the dark hallway and flew into the air only to land with a thud on the cold, hard, wood flooring.

When Mom narrated this story at family reunions Uncle Odie always half-heartedly chuckled, leading us to believe he never truly forgave his sisters.

As she morphed from a young farm girl into an undisciplined teen, Mom talked of becoming very disenchanted with living on a farm. "I remember sitting on the front porch swing just hoping a car would drive up the lane then, if one should arrive, I would pray for it to pull in. I was very lonely out on the farm."

On the occasions Mom did get to socialize, going to Lagro without chaperones was anticipated with gusto. This small town shaped many of the wonderful memories of Mom's teen years. Later, seeing her adolescent children heading out the door for an evening of fun, Mom would regale this particular pleasurable tale:

> Some summer nights, my girlfriends and I would go into the city of Lagro. In Lagro, which really only consisted of a block or two, there was a rock wall. We would buy our ice cream and then sit on this wall, slowly eating it. The young men from town would walk by and flirt. Then they would go around the block and walk by again. If we thought they were cute, we would stop them to talk.

According to Mom, this entertainment might go on for several hours, with many boys wandering by. This was a fun, casual way to spend a long, cicada-filled Indiana summer twilight.

Mom typically was enthusiastic when sharing stories about herself during her younger years, but she was reluctant to share the juicier details of her high school and college years, perhaps fearing her children would follow in her wild footsteps.

After Mom came to live with me, I returned once to Wabash to help clean out the family home. I came upon a small green book, with a broken lock it was Mom's diary. She had saved it all those years. Through handwritten pages, often in pencil, I was able to catch a glimpse of Mom in her rebellious young adult years.

The inside front cover read: *Received December 22, 1938, from Martha Ellen Miller, Lagro High School.* Mom was not a dedicated writer so there are many blank pages, but what did catch my eye is that almost every entry is about a date or a guy in which she was interested. Near the front of the book is a page entitled, "Boys I've gone out with." I counted. There were over fifty names.

Mom met many of her boyfriends during those summer evenings and pondered about them in her diary. Some of the boys were quite smitten with her. She wrote of more

35

than one young man who wanted to give her a ring, however, Mom was extremely interested in a particular guy named Joe Cooper.

*June 17, 1942*

*Dear Diary,*

*Heaven help me. I think I love Joe!! Really! I don't know though maybe I'm kidding myself, but I sure get a funny feeling when he kisses me.*

*June 21, 1942*

*Joe!!!!! And I do mean Joe!!!*

*July 3, 1942*

*Dear Diary,*

*Everything happens to me. Joe joined the Navy today. He leaves next Wednesday. Oh*

*diary, I don't know what I'll do. I'm used to*
*having him near. I'll miss him dreadfully.*


*July 8, 1942: I am so blue I can hardly write.*
*I went with Joe to Indianapolis and now he*
*is gone, gone... I feel like something has*
*been taken from me forever.*

There is evidence she saw Joe Cooper again before he

shipped out. My sister found pictures of Mom and a very

handsome young man in a Navy uniform on a Florida

beach. I assumed this was Joe Cooper. According to Odie's

wife, Mary, my grandfather gave her the money for the

trip because he liked Joe as he was a local boy and a

farmer. Joe isn't discussed much more in the diary after

this and it must be that Mom lost interest. Years later, I

discovered that Joe Cooper owned a local restaurant in

Wabash that my parents frequented. I often wondered

why

Mom joked about the owner's wife not being friendly.

Now I think I know the reason.

One of Mom's last diary entries mentions going off to college:

*August 28, 1942*

*Doris and I went to Ball State and rented the most adorable room today. We start school on the eighth.*

Left to right, back row, Mom, Betty,
front row, Odie, Maxine, Paul
circa 1930s

Mom on beach in Florida
1942

Mom
circa 1942/43

Mom in college
1940s

Mom high school senior portrait
she graduated April 24, 1942

Mom with boyfriend
1940s

Trees Mom read in
on the Family Farm

## College and Beyond

By all accounts from her siblings and friends, some of the greatest days of Mom's life were at Ball State University in Muncie, Indiana. While there her popularity with boys did not wane. She was a cheerleader, occasionally sang with a local band and she was involved with the drama club.

At one point during her college career Mom and her girlfriend, Tommy, decided to hitchhike across the country from Indiana to Washington State where Odie and Mary were stationed. This was a chancy, dangerous trip even by World War II standards when bumming rides from strangers was more acceptable.

Aunt Mary laughed, "No one knew they were going. They didn't even bother to tell their parents. They just left."

Years later, when the topic came up, Mom reluctantly told her impressionable daughters that she and Tommy hitched rides with truck drivers and families. When they ran out of money, the pair would wait tables, often not staying long enough to collect a paycheck, just the tips.

Odie was assigned to the Pasco Naval Air Station. On this base was a training school for new pilots, but another focus for the men was protection of a factory in the town of Richland. No one in the area knew what was being built in the factory; it was all very top secret. The plant opened in September 1944 and provided materials for producing the first atomic bombs. This top secret factory was part of what was eventually know as the Manhattan Project.

In recounting that era Aunt Mary said, "It wasn't until after we bombed Japan that they told us what the factory was for."

Life on the base proceeded as normally as possible during war times. According to Aunt Mary, Japan sent spy balloons over the west coast and the threat of being bombed was always present:

> While living on the base Mom and Tommy
> tried to be of help, but their good intentions
> did not always work out as planned. One

day, as they were walking home from the
grocery, the girls saw some very cute
soldiers washing jeeps and felt compelled to
stop and flirt. A couple of the guys offered
to carry their groceries home.

Mom's recollection of the story concurred with Aunt
Mary's version:

Imagine my horror when they put their
shirts back on and "P.O.W." was stamped in
bold letters on the back. These guys were
Italian prisoners of war. Odie and Mary
were furious with Tommy and me for
allowing them to walk us home.

Even though life did not always run smoothly between
the young couple and the two girls, Mom and Tommy
stayed with Odie and Mary for a quite awhile. Mary spoke
of this tumultuous time:

Housing on the base was sparse. You
basically got beds and a stove. Our kitchen
table was a cardboard box. Odie and I took

one of the beds and put it in the front room
as a daybed and Tommy and your Mom
stayed there. In order for me to get from
my bedroom to my babies' room, I had to
walk through the front room. I always gave
plenty of notice because you never knew
who was in the room or what was going on.
I didn't have any say about your Mom and
Tommy, they were adults, but we tried to
watch over them as best we could.

With the intent of more privacy, Mom and Tommy found
a trailer near the base and moved in. The quarters were
cramped, but enjoyed their freedom. When Odie was re-
stationed to the Coronado Island Base near San Diego for
the remainder of the war, Mom and Tommy decided to
follow the couple. Odie traveled with his troop while Mary
traveled alone by train, struggling with two young
children. Tommy and Mom hitchhiked. During their travels
south, the pair stayed for a while in a monastery. This is
where, according to rumors, Tommy had a tryst with a
priest. Eventually, the young wanderers landed in San

Diego and found jobs, but Mom said money was very tight. In order to supplement their incomes, both girls would find different dates to take them out for lunch and then dinner.

Mom laughed, remembering: "When the guys found out about each other, we had to start all over."

While the girls were in San Diego, the Allied Forces celebrated Victory in Europe Day on May 7, 1945. Mom told this thrilling story of the mayhem that took place between the celebrating public and soldiers:

> There were many uniformed men in town because they were either just shipping in or out. People were celebrating everywhere. Tommy and I were standing in a square near a fountain and guys would just come up and kiss us. Some were so forward that we had to run into a bathroom in the nearby bus station for safety.

With the war over, Odie was discharged from the Army. As Aunt Mary told the story:

When it was time to return home all four
of us left the base at the same time. Odie
and I and the babies took a nice,
respectable train ride. Your Mom and
Tommy hitchhiked. And even though they
were thumbing a ride, they beat us home!

Once back in Indiana, Mom returned to Ball State to
finish her schooling and get her Bachelor of Education
degree. She rarely related anecdotes about this part of her
life and I wish I knew more. I know she sang with a band
while in college, she always had a beautiful voice.

Mom often told her children, whenever a Glenn Miller
song came on the radio, of a memorable night at a concert
in Indianapolis where Tommy Dorsey and Glenn Miller
both performed:

Tommy Dorsey was at one end of the hall
and Glenn Miller was at the other. One
band would play, then, when they stopped,
the other band would pick up. I danced all
night with lots of different guys.

Mom met her future husband at one of these dances while she was in college. Years later, a sorority sister reminded Mom of the first time she danced with Joseph Thompson Christle.

> Corki, even though you were engaged to someone else you were dancing with Joe Christle. When I asked you who he was you just kept telling me, oh, I'm not interested in him, he's just a kid from home.

However, my Dad never forgot that night. As romantic thoughts revealed themselves in Dad's face, he reflected on the story of his first dance with Mom. He always said he noticed Mom because "she lit up the room."

Mom and her father, Harry Keffaber
on graduation from Ball State University
on August 16, 1946

Dad and Mom at her college graduation from Ball State
1946

Mom (second from left)
and the cheerleading squad from Ball State
(1942-46)

Mom and her girlfriend Mary Katherine Thomas
Mom always called her Tommy

Mom in college
as a cheerleader
on far left
1942-46

Mom and friend upon college
graduation from Ball State
1946

## A Chance on Marriage

Mom and Dad may have fallen in love, but my maternal grandfather was not pleased. He did not like Dad because he was a poor boy from the city of Wabash. Harry had every intention of his daughter marrying a rich farmer. Knowing they did not have the blessings of family, Mom and Dad eloped to Paducah, Kentucky on July 14, 1946. She wistfully remembered the beginning of their life together whenever our car approached the Indiana-Kentucky border on our family trips to Florida:

> Dad and I were madly in love, but your
> grandfather did not approve of Dad
> because he came from a very poor city
> family and was Catholic. I had been raised
> Christian Science, but converted to
> Catholicism during college before I met your
> dad. Because we knew my father would try
> to stop our marriage, we eloped to
> Paducah. Several of our friends came along

to be witnesses and to help us celebrate. At one point during the evening, they even managed to short sheet our wedding bed!

Mom and Dad spent about two weeks secretly married before they exchanged their vows in front of a priest. During those two weeks, they did not live as husband and wife, but would sneak out to Odie and Mary's farm. Aunt Mary laughingly recalled, "They always told us they had the sheets between them while in bed."

After their two weddings, Mom and Dad needed a place to live but funds were limited. Since my grandfather did not approve of the marriage, they could not ask him for help. Dad's family could only offer them space that Mom reluctantly agreed to. She had misgivings about moving into a house that she felt was male-dominated with Joe's three brothers, his father and his compliant mother. But Mom had no alternative. Later, Uncle Bob said with amusement, "Corki was a welcome addition to our family, we boys all loved her. She was a real spitfire. It took some getting used to though, as our household consisted mostly of men."

Mom remembers it also took Dad awhile to adjust to married life:

> On the first day I was living in his family's house, I waited all day for him to return from work. I was so happy he was home. Then I turned around and he was gone. My mother-in-law said 'well he always goes to the sweetshop after work.' I thought, *well, he didn't ask me to go*. So that was the beginning of husband training. But, he was always happy I made some changes. For one thing, his family was never affectionate. It was a long time before he could say 'I love you.' Then, he was always so happy he could hug me and say it.

In order to support themselves my parents bought a diner while Dad attended school. It was called The Avon. Dad would rise very early and go into prep the food. He became an expert on hamburger making, a technique of rounding the edges just right, that he passed on to me and, in turn, I passed to my daughters. Dad worked during the day and attended college in the evenings at Manchester University. While Dad attended class, Mom would pack baby Ranelle in a basket and take her to the diner so that she could clean in preparation for the next day.

Mom and Dad eventually relocated to a humble yet affordable apartment on Allen Street in Wabash, just a block from their diner. My mother would always smile thinking back on those days:

> Our apartment was very small. I used to
> hang clothes to dry over the kitchen table
> and we would sit down under them and eat
> dinner, but we were happy. Those were our
> happiest times. Dad was going to college on
> the GI Bill. He and a bunch of other ex-
> servicemen all rode up to Manchester
> together to attend classes. He had a ball.
> You know, he gave up four years of his
> youth but he never regretted it. He often

said, 'I sacrificed so that my kids will never have to deal with it.' He thought his generation had solved the world's problems with World War II so I thought of that after 9-11, and was glad he wasn't around to see that terrible day.

When Dad graduated, they sold the diner so that he could get a better job. He took a position as an insurance salesman for a small independent company. Always a people person, Dad excelled. He became one of the leading salesmen for the company. His work did not involve sitting in an office; instead, he traveled throughout the Midwest selling to groups. His main clients were city employees, teachers, firefighters and police officers. Mom also found a job and became infatuated with what would become her true professional calling, working with students.

After saving enough money and craving more space, Mom and Dad bought an older house in a crowded neighborhood on Miner Street in Wabash, just around the corner from Dad's family home. They happily took ownership. The family continued to grow until they had seven children over a time span of twenty years. Ranelle, Renita and Rhonda were either born or were toddlers while living on Miner Street.

   Mom and Dad, like many of their generation, were living the American Dream with their growing prosperity. After a few short years on Miner Street, they made the jump to a modern neighborhood on the outskirts of Wabash and, in 1957, purchased a three-bedroom-ranch for $19,000 on Bonbrook Drive. Mom and Dad lived there for the remainder of their married life. When they took ownership, the residence was under construction and not quite completed. In order to cut down on the cost of the house Dad, being a very capable handyman, finished the inside. One day while he installed cork tile in the living room, he got a phone call. The conversation turned into one of Dad's favorite stories:

      While I was working, the phone rang, so I answered it. My friend asked, 'What are you doing?' I said, 'Laying cork.' My friend became flustered and before abruptly hanging up the phone, he blurted out, 'Why the hell did you answer the phone?'

Dad's whole body shook with laughter when he told this story. He repeated it often and it developed into one of his favorite tales.

Remembering her days in the house on Miner Street where the kitchen window had looked out onto a brick wall, Mom had one condition for the new house:

> I told Dad I wanted a home with a window over the kitchen sink so that I could finally look out at the view and watch my children play.

Both Mom and Dad loved the house on Bonbrook Drive and took great pride in it. Over the years, Dad worked on finishing off the basement with a teen bedroom: a very large room with couches as beds and an old dining booth from the local American Legion, for playing games. He then added a rec room and his home office. The office consisted of a massive custom-made desk and a shelf that contained many of his awards for salesmanship. Mom and

Dad returned to this home from the hospital with their last four babies: me, Robin, Rocky and Tim.

With a flair for alliteration when naming their first six children, Ranelle, Renita, Rhonda, Rosemary, Robin and Roxann, many people questioned their choice when naming their first and only boy.

"Why the name Tim?"

Mom would always say, "Joe had waited a long time for a boy. We discussed naming Tim as Joe Jr., but we didn't like that. We came up with the idea of giving him Tim as his first name and Joseph as his middle name. Then their initials would be opposite of each other, JT and TJ."

Mom and Dad's first house on Miner Street in Wabash, Indiana

Mom and her favorite car enjoying more prosperous times
1960s

Early family photo
1960

Our home on Bonbrook Dr. in Wabash
1960s

## Family Life

When I was about five, Dad won an award for Salesman of the Year. The prize included two plane tickets to Colorado. Mom and Dad cashed in the tickets and instead of flying by themselves they drove and took the whole family. There were six girls at this time, ranging from toddlers to teens. Tim was still a dream away. Dad hitched a trailer to the car and we camped our way across Illinois, Missouri, Kansas and into Colorado.

The trip did not go without incident. Mom spent days packing the trailer. She stocked it with the food and staples she would need to cook over a campfire for eight people. On the first night after an exhaustive day on the road, we stopped to set up camp and opened the door of the trailer. With flour dust still settling like remnants of a bomb blast, Mom found the interior of the camper coated with the white powder. The five-pounds of flour had seeped into every crack, covered the floor and coated our beds. The combination of the swaying of the trailer and the cupboards not being properly locked had resulted in catastrophe. Mom, with resilience and relying on her two oldest daughters, put Renita in charge of the younger children while she and Ranelle cleaned up the mess. The entire fiasco was a climatic ending to the first day of our family trip.

After several more days of travel, including shoes lost in a roaring creek, and long days spent in a cramped car with too few bathroom breaks, our family finally reached our destination: The Broadmoor Hotel in Colorado Springs.

Exhausted, the true challenge for my Mom was about to begin.

Upon our arrival, Mom had to get all six girls clean enough to enter a five star hotel, no simple task from inside a small trailer without a shower. Mom had an image in mind of heads turning with coos of wonderment as her beautiful family entered the Broadmoor Hotel lobby. To prepare for our initial appearance Mom spent many long evenings, along with Dad's Aunt Hilda, stitching together brown plaid matching cotton dresses and an identical print shirt for Dad. With a week's worth of camping dirt embedded in us, Mom bathed each younger girl one by one and then helped us into our finery. After being scrubbed clean and dressed, we were instructed to stand outside the trailer and not touch anything. Oh, how my older sisters hated those outfits. However, Mom and Dad were proud of their brood and with grand smiles they marched us all in. I don't recall many other details of that trip, but the family portrait, later made into a Christmas card is priceless. I also have pictures of Mom and Dad, the joy and pride reflected on their faces, as they are crowned the King and Queen of the banquet. The long arduous journey was worth all the effort.

Upon return to Wabash, our family life underwent some major changes. Ranelle entered her freshman year at Purdue University in West Lafayette, Indiana, and Mom and Dad soon welcomed Tim to the family. With the added stress of a new baby, college tuition, and the ever-demanding needs of a large family, my father started turning more to a vice that had been trickling into his daily life for years: alcohol. For many years to come this disease would haunt him, our family and Mom and Dad's relationship.

When Tim was still a toddler and in order to make ends meet, Mom returned to teaching. She found a position as an English teacher at the local junior high. With combined incomes, an assortment of loans and work-study programs, Mom and Dad managed to send all seven of their children to college. To maintain a balanced budget they often struggled to find money for household items and clothing. We younger children ran barefoot all summer. On the days, Mom paid bills she spent hours sorting through and deciding which ones she should pay, and which could wait. At the end of the month when money ran low, we ate a lot of ham and beans for dinner. Always, just under the surface, were the sparks of discontent that ran between my parents because of Dad's increased drinking. They argued frequently. Mom often had one of us call the American Legion, where Dad spent his afternoons, to ask the bartender to send him home for dinner. Despite Dad's drinking, he continued working at his insurance sales position.

Christmas photo
1964

Family portrait
1968

Family portrait
1985

Another sibling off to Purdue University
1967

Dad winning a company award
Early 1960s

Our matching outfits for our Broodmoor Hotel debut
1963

## A Life Well Spent

Mom and Dad became well known in the community of Wabash; Dad through his business and Mom by means of her teaching. My siblings and I, with the guidance and example of our parents, became involved in student organizations, sports, and theater and one by one, left to attend college.

Mom worked hard at being a good mother knowing the void she felt after her mother died. On summer nights that were too hot to climb into sticky sheets, we sat on the back steps as Mom read to us. My sister, Rhonda, recalls those evenings as her favorite:

> I remember snuggling next to Mom
> spellbound as she read to me the big book
> of *Best Loved Poems.* Her voice was like
> warm tea and honey, sweet and soothing,
> yet alive with bursts of highly spiced
> expression. "The Raggedy Man" and "Little
> Orphan Annie" by James Witcomb Riley, an

Indiana poet, were two of Mom's favorites. She knew them by heart and would perform the poems in her best Hoosier accent. Part of the charm of those poems is the repetition of the ending stanzas. I would anticipate them in thrilled suspense as she paused and slowed her voice and eerily said, 'An the Gobble-uns at gits you, Ef you don't' watch out!' Or I would giggle with sheer delight as Mom exclaimed, 'Raggedy! Raggedy! Raggedy Man!'

Camping was a pastime that my parents could afford and one that we children relished. For several summers, Dad pulled our trailer out to the local state campground built on a bluff overlooking the Salamonie Reservoir, just twenty minutes from our home. The family spent weeks at a time living there. Dad went to work in the morning, leaving Mom in charge.

The Christle kids explored, hiked, fished, and kept occupied all day. One of our favorite activities was swinging over steep ravines from skinny vines that looked like long snakes slithering through the air. One summer, to our delight, Dad found an old canoe and brought it to the campsite. Many countless hot, muggy days were spent paddling around the calm, muddy brown water filled with jumping and croaking frogs.

Mom's favorite pastime was to fish. She typically sat alone on a rock beside a tranquil cove, a cane pole cradled between her legs. When we children happened upon her, she made us sit still so as not to disturb the fish. Eventually, we grew bored and wandered away, leaving Mom to what she wanted all along: peace and quiet.

While camping, another form of family entertainment was sitting around the campfire and singing. Mom would lead and her sunburned, wood-smoked choir would follow. We sang favorites from her younger days: "Tell Me Why the Sky's So Blue," "Shanty in Ole Shanty Town," "Down by the Old Mill Stream," and "Slide Down My Cellar Door." Mom always included a song just for Tim, "Mama's Little Fellow", which caused all us girls to squirm with jealousy.

One summer, when my sister Ranelle brought a boyfriend to the campground, Mom wanted to make sure he felt welcomed. At home, in anticipation, she spent an afternoon making her special recipe of spaghetti sauce. She then froze it knowing that, while camping, it had to be stored in a cooler for a few days. When Ranelle and her guest arrived, Mom put her frozen masterpiece in a big pot, to let it gradually thaw over the campfire. As the tomato red globe was melting, and Mom and Dad were getting to know Ranelle's beau, a thunderstorm swiftly began racing across the reservoir. We all scattered for cover in the trailer or cars as huge streaks of lightning, deafening claps of thunder, and rolling dark clouds descended upon us.

Thrown about by the wind the trees began to shake and bend, and the pot over the fire began to dance.

"Oh, no!" Mom cried out, her heart dropping with the realization that dinner had been left behind over the campfire. In that instant, a gust of wind swept down and tossed the pot onto the ground. The sauce, still frozen, rolled across the dirt and came to rest up against a tree.

We all watched with empty stomachs in dismay. As quickly as the storm had come up, it moved on. Mom rushed out of the trailer, picked up the ball of frozen sauce and accumulated muck and calmly rinsed off the inedible portion and stuck it back in the pot to finish cooking. It seemed normal to our family; this was all we had for dinner.

We often laughed about Ranelle's date wondering what he must have thought.

Mom always loved chocolate in any form. One Valentine's Day, when my two younger sisters and I were in high school, we were feeling forlorn. Sadly, none of us had received a heart-shaped box full of bon-bons. Seeing our distress and wanting an excuse to eat chocolate, Mom took control of the matter. She handed over the car keys and directed me to purchase Valentine's Day sweets at Gackenheimer's, the local pharmacy. Upon my return, with enthusiasm and delight, all of us dove into the wide assortment of chocolates. Too soon, the box was empty. We looked at each other, the last morsels still melting in our mouths. Without a word, Mom handed me the keys and off I went again for another box.

During Mom's career as an educator, she moved from the junior high to teach at the high school. This suited her, as she preferred working with older teenagers. Her classes quickly became the popular ones. She enjoyed all of her students, but her favorites were the underdogs. Mom developed into the champion of the little guy, guiding them with her experience and direction. The administration realized Mom's gift and offered to appoint her high school counselor. She accepted. Part of the deal required Mom to get a counseling degree. With this decision, our family routine changed dramatically. Mom would come home from school after an exhausting day of teaching to take a short nap. Rising, the educator, now transformed into student, grabbed a meal cooked by me, as I was the oldest child at home. She then drove for over an hour to her night classes where the sessions went late. Mornings came early. She started each day as mother, getting her children off to school and then herself to work. It paid off. Mom kept her appointment as counselor in the profession she loved.

My siblings and I still hear from close friends and, at times, even strangers about how our mother helped them through very difficult times. Out of respect for her students, Mom kept conversations confidential. Sometimes the very person she was counseling might be sitting at our dinner table that night, invited over as just a friend. Rhonda went to a class reunion and was captivated by a classmate who told this story:

> Your mother was very dear to me. I got in trouble in high school and ended up in jail. Your mom was the only person who came to visit me there. She sat with me until late in the night. Another time, when I got pregnant, your mom counseled me and tried to offer me alternatives to giving up my baby - the only option the priest and my mother insisted upon.

My youngest sister, Rocky, heard this from a neighborhood friend:

> I was struggling in high school with some real emotional issues. Your mom spoke with

me, sometimes daily, and helped me
through my crisis.

Although I don't know many details, after Mom retired
she worked with battered women at The Women's Shelter
in town. There she used her counseling and teaching
degrees to help the women who found themselves at this
junction in their lives. According to a friend of Mom's,
there was one night that was a particularly dangerous and
desperate situation:

> I remember once when Corki had to take
> a girl to Kokomo, a town about an hour
> away. She had Joe go with her because the
> girl's boyfriend had beaten her so badly
> they were afraid he would follow them and
> cause more trouble.

Mom rarely mentioned her work with the shelter, in
order to protect the women she assisted.

After years of helping others, Mom finally realized her
own marital relationship was in dire need of an
intervention. Sometime around 1980, Mom informed Dad

that he must either stop drinking or move out of the house. Because he loved Mom and didn't want to lose her, Dad promised to quit. At first, he struggled to keep his promise to her, but eventually he succeeded in conquering his demons. Dad did not drink alcohol for the remainder of his life. This was certainly an admirable feat and one that was greatly appreciated by his family.

Christmas morning
1968

Mom in her favorite fishing spot
with our dog, Penney

Dad's birthday
1970s

Camping at Salamonie Reservoir
1970s

Mom and Dad
1960

**Retirement Years**

With all of their children out of the nest and Dad's issues with alcohol behind them, Mom and Dad settled into retirement. They enjoyed traveling around the country to visit their now grown children and families. Dad ran for the City Court Judge (a position that does not require a law degree in the state of Indiana), and was elected. He held the title until his death on February 21, 2001. Within days of Dad's passing, Governor Frank O'Bannon's office contacted Mom and asked if she would be interested in taking her husband's place on the bench, an appointment only a governor is allowed to make. Mom was startled, but honored.

A day or two after the funeral, an aide to Governor O'Bannon arrived at our home. Because there were so many of us sleeping and eating in the small ranch house, I remember it was a mess. We tried to tidy up as best we could, hiding suitcases and stashing pillows into corners. When the aide arrived at the door, several of us hurried our small children to the basement in hopes of allowing Mom a more dignified introduction. He looked around at the sea of faces staring at him, seemed to hesitate, then gathered his courage and walked into the crowded living room. Someone pushed coffee and dessert onto his lap as he nervously took a seat near Mom. After asking her a few polite questions, he then formally presented Mom with the Governor's request. With a smile on her lips and sadness in her eyes, Mom accepted.

It took a few more weeks to complete the FBI background checks and to obtain final approval. Mom took office in March of 2001. On the bench, she once again sought to help those struggling with the overwhelming realities of life. She now served sentences on those downtrodden citizens she had spent her adult life advocating for. Mom often found it difficult to pass judgment on plaintiffs not paying rent. When she questioned them as to why they had not done so they sometimes explained, "We can't afford to pay for our medical expenses and rent. Sometimes we have to make a choice."

Many times Mom offered the choice of a job or jail time. She would help those who were interested in finding employment, always going the extra step for those in need.

Mom ran on the Democratic ticket, but lost her bid for re-election in 2003. For the first time in her adult life, Mom did not have a career or family to focus on. It was at this point my siblings and I noticed a change in Mom. We struggled to help her from afar, most of us living many states away, as far as Oregon, Georgia, Florida and New York. Rocky and I, on numerous occasions, flew in to help Mom at home. We took her to doctor appointments, cleaned her house, and stocked the refrigerator and cupboards. We hired help to come in, which Mom would promptly fire after our visits. Her children, on more than one occasion, tried to convince her to move into one of their homes. Mom's typical reply was, "I am not leaving this house unless it is feet first."

Mom's friends from Bridge group and her book club also became concerned. When asked, Mom always maintained that she was doing fine when, in reality, the threads of her life due to the onset of dementia, were beginning to unravel.

And so, in May of 2006, approximately five years after the death of her husband of fifty-five years, I flew to Wabash with the intent of bringing Mom back to Clifton Park, New York, to live with me. In this manner, we began our final journey.

Mom and Dad
renewing vows
1996

Mom with several of her grandchildren
1992

Mom, my children Catlin and Kristen, Dad
at our home in Clifton Park, NY
Easter morning 1991

Dad and Mom
enjoying their sunroom
2000

Dad and Mom in their retirement fun car
1996

Mom and Dad visiting in Portland, Oregon
1996

Dad and Mom in Maine
1990

Mom and Dad with grandchildren
1993

Oregon Coast at the wreck of the Peter-Iredale

Mom and Dad swooning over another grandchild
1991

Mom's swearing in day
April 3, 2001

Judge Christle and grandchildren after a court visit
2002

**Part II**

**Mom Moves In**

    The process of getting Mom to leave Wabash was several years long; it began soon after she lost her bid for re-election in 2003.

    All of Mom's children kept tabs on her, but Rocky and I checked in more than the others. There were many reasons for this. Ranelle had some health issues of her own and worked full time. Renita, Rhonda and Robin lived on the west coast; because of the time difference, making phone calls to Mom was difficult. Rhonda was also consumed with her own health problems. Tim lived minutes away yet couldn't bring himself to admit the gravity of Mom's declining mental health - a reality that was hard for all seven of us to bear. Although rearing young children of our own, neither Rocky nor I had jobs that required a daily commitment making it easier for us to travel. I think Mom understood her children's issues and knew she could rely on Rocky and me.

Mom had always been very attentive to getting whatever she needed done, accomplished with precision and accuracy. On the days she ran her errands, for example, Mom planned her route so that she only made right hand turns, thus not losing time waiting for traffic. As time went on, we all began to notice changes in the way Mom performed her daily activities. There were more than a few indications this was not the mother we had all grown up with. When asked specific questions about the upkeep of the house or her daily life, Mom became flustered and confused. When we pushed for more information, she would simply switch the subject. We all believed Mom was lonely, overwhelmed from taking care of her home and consumed by her increasing medical appointments. Mom, being stubborn would never ask for help.

A typical conversation with her at this time went something like this:

"Mom, would it make you feel better if I came to some of your appointments with you?"

"I don't know. I suppose. A friend from Bridge group could drive me, but her driving makes me nervous."

"Mom, I'll fly out. We could have some fun, too."

"Well, it would be nice, but I hate to ask."

It was the same scenario for Rocky. When either of us visited, we sat in on the appointments trying to make sense of what was going on with Mom's overall health. As Mom's calls and our visits became more frequent, Rocky and I decided our new course of action would be to convince her to move in with one of her children.

Together, we planned a trip in the summer of 2006 to visit Mom and stay for a week. We did our usual household cleaning and visits to doctors with Mom. Mid-week, Rocky and I took Mom to Manchester, the same small town where Dad attended college to get a breaded tenderloin sandwich at Dave's, our favorite little diner. We did not share that we also planned a stop at an assisted living community. Lunch was great and Mom enjoyed getting out of the house. As we left, Rocky and I sprang the news on Mom of our next destination. Mom was leery; she had a fear of "nursing homes."

As we pulled out of the diner's parking lot she adamantly stated, "I would rather die first before living in a nursing home."

"Mom, just take a look at this place, you might be surprised," I said, hoping my voice did not portray the confidence I lacked. We were answered with silence.

To get to the entrance we drove down an extended driveway through a manicured landscape. I dropped Rocky and Mom off under the covered breezeway before parking the car. The three of us entered a large formal foyer with oriental rugs and a huge vase full of seasonal flowers placed on a table that was centered in the middle of the room. The director cordially met us and he gave us a tour. As we walked the hallways, we were pleasantly surprised to encounter many people that Mom knew from Wabash. The home had a large living room where we watched a child and grandmother playing the piano together. There were windows everywhere looking onto lovely old trees surrounded with multi-colored flowerbeds. The hallways were carpeted and glowed with the warmth of low lighting. The cafeteria had formal tablecloths and napkins. Lunch smelled wonderful. Towards the end of our tour, we were guided from the main building to the stand-alone patio homes. These small homes had one or two bedrooms, kitchen, laundry, and living room all with a cozy floor plan designed for easy mobility. The patio homes were so lovely, I wanted to move in. It was obvious Mom was impressed and aware that her idea of a "nursing home" and this community differed greatly. Once we were all back in the car, though, she stuck out her bottom lip and put on a stern face.

I started the conversation.

"Mom, what did you think?"

"It is a nice place, but I already have a home and I plan on staying there."

"But Mom, here you would have someone to cook and clean for you and there would be other people around to play bridge and watch TV with."

It was obvious there would be no more discussion of the move as Mom turned her head to look out the passenger window and, again, gave us the silent treatment.

Disappointed, Rocky and I shifted to Plan B. We got Mom a call-alert necklace and set up payment for the service. We interviewed a local woman and hired her to help Mom by doing her laundry, cooking and cleaning. Rocky and I bought a medication dispenser. It was huge and divided into morning, noon, afternoon, and night slots. We asked Mom's aide to fill the dispenser each week and to make sure Mom was taking her prescriptions. Content that we could do nothing more, we packed our suitcases and flew back home to our neglected families.

Only a few short days after we left, Mom told her aide she didn't need her on daily basis. Then Mom insisted she didn't need her to cook or do laundry. Finally, Mom said she didn't need her at all.

Sadly, we were back to Mom being alone.

Feeling frustrated, Rocky and I came up with another plan, one we were trying to avoid. We would have to try tough love. We explained to Mom that we could not continue flying in to assist her. I know she felt hurt and it was difficult for Rocky and me to do; Mom required help daily and we hoped that leaving her on her own for a while would hasten this realization.

Over the following winter, hearing frightening stories, all of us were even more convinced that Mom could no longer live alone. We learned Mom had fallen at her home several times, once waking up on the cold cement garage floor. Another time, while wandering in the middle of the night, she fell in her living room. She telephoned Tim for help and instead of coming to her house; he stayed on the phone until she crawled across the floor and pulled herself onto the couch.

When questioned later as to why she didn't use her call-alert necklace, Mom said, "I didn't want to bother the company."

My siblings and I agreed these were troubling signs. Yet, Mom's daily life was far worse than we knew. We eventually learned that Mom was living on cans of beans and chocolate Ensure. That she no longer communicated with her friends, went to book club or played Bridge. We discovered on one occasion when a friend came over to check on her, Mom wouldn't let her in the house, slamming the door. Contrary to what was actually happening, when family called, Mom talked about playing Bridge or the book she was reading. She chatted about driving to the movie rental store and the grocery. She was convincing! An intelligent woman, Mom cleverly disguised her daily life, repeating to us what she had done months ago, not what she did the day before. Consequently, she easily hid her ever-increasing signs of becoming a recluse.

During the early spring of 2007, there were the beginnings of signs that Mom was having a change of heart about help. Mom kept calling me to solve problems with her house or perhaps settle a bill. The calls were unusual because she typically never called; Mom had always waited for her children to dutifully call her.

After one of her recurring phone calls I nonchalantly asked, "Mom, why don't you come visit me and my family? It would be fun."

"Well, I think I might. It sounds nice."

I was stunned when Mom readily agreed. This was a clear sign to me that she was struggling on her own. Mom told me the trip was a chance to see her daughter and granddaughters. I had a nagging feeling in my heart that Mom needed more help than she was willing to admit.

I hung up the phone that Sunday afternoon and found my husband, Paul, sitting at his desk in his office. He looked up from his keyboard.

"How is your Mom?"

"She's coming to visit us," I said with a slight smile, hoping that would let Paul know I was surprised Mom said yes. The room became still as we locked eyes at the realization that one short conversation was about to change our world.

Paul spoke first. "You realize, once she gets here she will likely never be able to leave."

This was a topic we had loosely discussed in the past and vaguely agreed that we could handle. We knew having Mom move in with us was the right thing to do for her.

I said with false hope, "Well, she claims it is only for a visit, so we will see. I think once she gets around people who love and care for her she will rebound to her old self."

At dinner that evening, we had a family conversation with our youngest daughter, Kristen. She was finishing up her junior year in high school. She welcomed the visit from Grammy Cork, as she and her sister Catlin called my Mom. We all agreed it would be nice for my mother to have a chance to get to know our family better since the distance over several states had always prevented her participation in our family routine.

The life Paul and I shared with our daughters was wonderfully hectic. In the summer months, we spent many days boating and camping on Lake George in the Adirondack Park of northern New York. Our winters were even busier. At one point both our girls raced competitively for their high school and the Gore Mountain downhill ski teams. The schedule had eased somewhat as Catlin was enjoying her freshman year at Purdue University. However, Kristen's skiing schedule included many weekends of practice at Gore Mountain and travel to other race locations.

Optimistically we concluded, if we had to travel for a race, why couldn't Mom come along? In the winter, she could stay at our rental house, near Gore Mountain and read books until we returned from skiing for the day. How wonderful it would be for Mom to picnic with us on Lake George in the summer. We called Catlin and discussed the fact that her grandmother would be visiting and perhaps living with us during the summer months when she would be back home. Catlin liked the idea. As a family, we were all hopeful that Mom's visit, and likely extended stay, would be fun for all of us. Over the next few days, I dreamed of heart-to-heart talks and sage advice from Mom, forming a bond Mom and I never quite established.

So it was, naively perhaps, that we welcomed the thought of my mother moving in with us.

It was early April. Paul and I had a Caribbean cruise planned for later in the month. I told Mom I would fly out to visit her for a few days during the first week of May. I planned to squeeze the trip between the cruise and

Kristen's junior prom. I mentioned I would help her pack some things and, since Mom hated to fly, I promised I would drive her in her beloved bright red Lincoln Town Car back to my home in upstate New York.

I planned an extended visit in Wabash. I hoped Mom and I could visit my cousins. I was anxious to savor some of the local food I missed while living in upstate New York. I craved a breaded pork tenderloin sandwich, or maybe a Spanish (a family kept recipe for a meat sauce) hotdog, and a frosted mug of root beer from the local A&W. I wanted to visit the Salamonie Reservoir where we had camped as a family and I thought it would be fun to drive around to my old high school haunts.

I arrived at the Indianapolis Airport, rented a car and drove to my childhood home on Bonbrook Drive in Wabash. As I pulled the car into the driveway and parked, I realized it was already warm for a day in May. As I walked up the sidewalk, I could smell the fertilizer being spread on the fields just outside of town. My nose crinkled and I sucked in and held my breath so I wouldn't smell the ripe aroma of manure in the air. When I stepped onto the porch, I expected to see Mom at the door. Instead, I had to let myself in. There she sat in a dark living room. I glanced around remembering the many family pictures taken in front of the salmon pink limestone fireplace that filled the wall at the far end of the living room. I looked for the family portraits and my wedding picture. I waited for the years of childhood memories to come flooding back but they did not, could not, as I looked at my mother. She looked frail, tired and scared. Her clothing was dirty and covered with stains. I was taken aback. *How had my mother let herself get to this state?* Mom always took pride in her appearance. She had dressed competently as a high school counselor, later professionally as the city court judge. Now she wore clothing that did not match. Food had dribbled down the front of her shirt. Seeing her this way terrified me. I took a deep breath; I struggled not to appear shocked. Mom seemed embarrassed by the way she looked and the mess the house was in. I quivered with the gradual realization she was no longer capable of performing these daily tasks.

When she mentioned on the phone she couldn't pack her suitcase I assumed it was not that she couldn't, but that she didn't want to. I quickly realized she didn't have the stamina or the capability to decide what to pack. Our past phone conversations raced through my mind and I concluded she must have been lying to me about her lifestyle. I attributed her current condition to depression about my father's death and losing her bid for re-election.

Instead of traipsing the familiar places of my youth, I spent four days visiting Mom's doctors, getting her car in working order, throwing out rancid food and packing for Mom. She sat on her bed and weakly told me which articles of clothing she might want to bring along. Most of her clothes were not clean so I stuffed them in a suitcase. Just going through her medications was overwhelming. There were many duplicate prescriptions, some unopened bottles, and others were empty with no renewals. I was frustrated trying to decipher what prescriptions Mom actually needed to take and why.

Over the next few days, I felt besieged with decisions about Mom. On the outside I was the picture of efficiency. Inside, I was emotionally falling apart.

With grave clarity, I realized that Mom was now the child and I, the parent.

On the last day, I helped Mom climb into her packed Lincoln. We pulled down the driveway passing the flagpole where Dad always displayed his favorite flags. She barely glanced at our home, the one I had grown up in, literally since birth. Swallowing my tears and putting on a brave face for Mom, I quietly drove Mom away.

Mom and Kristen
on prom night
2006

## Bringing Mom to New York

Mom and I drove straight through to my home in upstate New York. We stopped for lunch and bathroom breaks, but I understood Mom would not be comfortable in a hotel and, frankly, I knew neither one of us would get any sleep. I worried she would fall or become disoriented and Mom would have just been anxious. I drove the twelve hours with the cruise control at seventy-three miles per hour. The thing drove like a boat and we sailed over potholes and around other cars through the flatlands of Indiana and Ohio, where visibility is clear for miles ahead. We made our way in and out of Pennsylvania quickly and arrived on the western edge of New York State, anticipating the rolling green hills and the beautiful lake shore that runs parallel to Interstate 90.

The Lincoln's soft, worn leather seats comforted Mom as she recalled her many days of travel with my father. Strangely, I noticed she waved to all of the truckers. Normally, in years past, she always spoke of how much she hated the big semis hogging the road, making so much noise.

"Mom, why are you waving to all of the truckers?"

"Well, they just seem lonely and work so hard, driving all the time."

*Okay*, I thought. *That is new*. Mom continued waving throughout our journey and the anticipation of her next "hello" kept her occupied.

Finally, we pulled into my driveway, Mom was probably anticipating a visit; I was hoping to return her to the woman I once knew. It is my nature to "fix" problems and I naively thought I could fix Mom.

Before my rescue mission, many discussions transpired between my siblings and me about Mom's care. Rocky and I, along with Paul and our daughters, had imagined that Mom's issues could be solved by simply moving her into a nourishing environment where she was surrounded by loved ones.

I believed Mom needed to return to a routine of eating normally and getting her medications on schedule. We were convinced she would then evolve back into the woman we knew and missed. However, after a few short weeks, it became apparent Mom's condition was far more complicated and the living arrangement was going to be more difficult than anticipated.

In the beginning, we felt confident that we could nurse Mom back to health. The first weeks were difficult and each day would bring a new obstacle. Mom was no longer accustomed to eating at regular intervals. She wanted to continue drinking Ensure as her main diet. Mom's sleep regimen was a constant battle. The mornings were long and drawn out. On a typical morning, I would get up with Kristen and have coffee while she got ready for school and ate her breakfast. Once she left, I spent the morning checking emails, cleaning up the house, and doing laundry. Eventually around 10:00 a.m., I would start to wake Mom. Some days I got her out of bed after the first or second attempt. Other days, it took me more than an hour to coax her from beneath the blankets. Mom's grumbling and whining about our established routines became more frequent.

Our conversations were the same morning after morning.

"Mom, it's a beautiful day today. You should get up."

Without opening her eyes, Mom would complain, "I don't see what is so beautiful about it."

"Well, the sun is shining and the birds are singing."

"Who cares? I just want to sleep, and I hurt all over."

"I have coffee made, and I can make you some breakfast."

"I don't want any."

Then she would pull the blankets over her head, dismissing me. Frustrated, I would leave, wander downstairs, occupy myself for a while and then return later to begin the task all over again.

By the time Mom came down for breakfast I was always hungry for lunch. Most days I made her a cup of coffee and brought it to her while she sat in our family room watching CNN. I would eat my lunch at the kitchen table where I could keep an eye on Mom. There was never conversation between us, only silence. While sipping her coffee with cream and sugar I observed as Mom gradually hatched from her cocoon. The first few days I made her breakfast but she argued over the fact that she didn't want any. Eventually, I gave up and started serving Mom lunch about an hour after I helped her down the stairs. It took me several weeks to wean her from a liquid diet to eating solid foods. I enticed her with her favorite meals. I cooked meatloaf, mashed potatoes, fried chicken and more mashed potatoes, this time with gravy. For dessert, it was pies or ice-cream, or both. Fat and calories were thrown to the wayside. To keep sane and minimize the kitchen work, I served the meals to my whole family. Paul and the girls complained about the non-healthy dishes. Mom whined saying she wasn't hungry and shouldn't be forced to eat. Frustrated, I said nothing and silently ate the fattening meals and gained weight.

At night, we reversed our argument about going to sleep. I needed to be in bed early and Mom wanted to stay up late and watch *Late Show with David Letterman*. I knew she would not stay downstairs without me so I would simply stand and prepare to go upstairs while she protested about the early bedtime. As we made our way up the stairs, I had Mom climb in front of me. I grasped the railings on both sides with a firm grip, hoping that if she fell, my body would act as a shield and prevent her from falling down the full flight of stairs.

A huge dilemma for Paul and me was the fact that we could no longer go out on short notice with friends. We were nervous about leaving Mom at home alone. We had to plan days in advance with either Catlin or Kristen to stay home with their Grammy Cork.

Understanding our predicament, neighbors invited us along with Mom to their home for dinner. It was a lovely, warm spring evening and they planned a cookout. We drove Mom the half a block to their house. I helped her from the backseat. Approaching the front door, I had Mom by the arm, or so I thought. As she stepped onto the porch, she missed and fell, bloodying her knee and knocking out two teeth. The scene was devastating. I felt I had not protected Mom. Paul felt he should have been helping Mom and me by supporting her other side, and our neighbors felt somehow responsible for the whole fiasco.

That wasn't the only time Mom fell and I quickly learned to keep a firmer grip on her. Mom's balance was off, she wobbled as she walked and wheezed with exertion. Every time she had to make the small step from our family room to the kitchen, I held my breath as I watched her struggle and lean on the railing to pull herself up.

Mom gained strength as she transitioned from protein shakes to a more traditional diet. The socialization with my family allowed her face to brighten. I thought I could return to substitute teaching. Paul had a home office and, when not traveling, spent his days there. We determined that Paul could attend to Mom's needs until I returned home around 2:30 p.m. to resume her care

Our plan did not last long. Mom became disoriented without me. Upon waking, she would call for me and become frightened when I did not appear, thinking she was alone in the house. Paul often had to hang up on business calls to calm her down. This conflict was a struggle for Paul and an interference with his job. On more than one occasion, I came home to find Mom still in bed. I would have to coax her to get dressed and eat something. Her medication schedule was in disarray on the days I worked. The stress leaving Mom was simply not worth the effort, nor the money, so I quit.

Mom and I went back to our routine of arguing about getting in and out of bed. She also began to complain she was bored. Going into my fix-it mode, I investigated the local senior citizens center and arranged for Mom to join an existing Bridge group.

"Mom, I found a place for you to play Bridge. You said you were bored."

"I can't play Bridge without my cardholders; I have too much arthritis in my fingers and I can't hold the cards."

"Mom, I got you cardholders, now you can play Bridge." A frown creased her face.

"I will drive you over tomorrow and walk you in; I can even stay if you want me to."

She mumbled, "Okay."

The next morning Mom refused to get out of bed, said she was sick, and couldn't play Bridge that day. After several encouraging attempts it occurred to me that wasn't that Mom didn't want to play, maybe she couldn't play anymore.

I dropped the idea and moved on.

I rented movies or we sat on the back deck and enjoyed the outdoors, something Mom hadn't done in years. But, I felt trapped in my house. I couldn't run errands unless someone was home with Mom or she was sleeping. She became very dependent on me and would panic unless I was within her view. Understanding my frustration, friends stopped by to chat so that I could enjoy some socialization.

As spring waned into summer, I faced another dilemma. Mom was comfortable in my home but did not like to venture out. Our family looked forward to our summer practice, boating on Lake George. I was torn between the guilt of breaking our family tradition or dragging my Mom somewhere she didn't feel comfortable. The responsibility of caring for Mom was taking its toll on all of us. As a family, we had envisioned sharing our life with Mom as a positive endeavor. We battled our preconceived notions of an idyllic life with Mom with the reality that Mom's issues were far grimmer than depression and old age.

### Realization Sets In

During my time as a substitute teacher, I became
acquainted with women who were struggling with similar
caretaker dilemmas. We compared notes on finding help
with the many different issues of caring for an elderly
loved one. Over time, we formed bonds as we
commiserated. We smiled knowingly at each other as we
passed in the hallways. One woman was dealing with
finding care not only for her mother, but for her aunt as
well. In her desperation to remain working full-time and
care for her them, she had compiled a list of hairdressers,
local transportation, aides, and a doctor, all of whom
made house calls. She graciously shared her list with me
and I will be forever grateful for her organization and
generosity. At this point, I felt I could still take Mom out
for most appointments, but a geriatric doctor who made
house calls - this was a find! Knowing, he wasn't accepting
new patients, I called Dr. Cee anyway and pleaded our
case into his answering machine. I was desperate. Because
he was a kind man, Dr. Cee agreed to see Mom. He soon
became a crucial figure in our lives.

During his visits, Dr. Cee and I discussed Mom's symptoms and he gave her simple cognitive and memory tests. We talked about how Mom had changed from the woman I knew to the one living in my house now. Gradually, Dr. Cee made me aware that Mom's issues were more than depression. The symptoms she had were more than old age, even though she was in her eighties. At one point, as he packed up his scale securing it to his traveling bag with bungee cords, he spoke the words that were already forming in the back of my mind.

Dr. Cee looked me straight in the eye and said with compassion, "I believe your mother has some form of dementia."

I nodded in agreement and my tears silently flowed as Mom sat oblivious to the situation, watching re-runs of *Seinfeld*.

Dr. Cee advised us to see Dr. Zimmer, a local specialist on dementia. Before our initial visit, his office requested all of Mom's past medical records. It took me several weeks, but I managed to have them sent from her primary care doctor and her heart specialist back in Indiana. Accompanying the information from the cardiologist, I found a DVD of a scan of Mom's brain. It seemed odd to me her cardiologist had ordered this test, but he had seen Mom for years and may have noticed symptoms that concerned him about possible dementia. I took the DVD with me to our first appointment.

My stress level was incredibly high as I struggled with the realization that the Dr. Zimmer would tell me what I already knew. To complicate matters, Mom and I got lost in the expanse of The Medical Center and arrived way behind our scheduled appointment time. Thankfully, Dr. Zimmer was also running late. Unfortunately, this gave Mom the time to peruse her surroundings and realize we were visiting a dementia specialist. The doctor took time to examine Mom, running through many of the same cognitive tests Dr. Cee had already used. Dr. Zimmer seemed intrigued. As an afterthought he said, "Let's take a look at that DVD."

We moved to a large conference room, followed by Dr. Zimmer's impatient nurse and an intern. Dr. Zimmer threw the DVD into his computer and the image jumped onto a large screen in the front of the room. A gasp went through all gathered, except Mom. The doctor, nurse, intern, and I, even with my untrained eye, all saw the huge void in the front of Mom's brain. I was stunned.

Dr. Zimmer contemplated the image quietly before he confidently stated, "Given your mother's symptoms and this picture, I would say she has Temporal Frontal Lobe Dementia."

"How is that different from Alzheimer's?"

"There are some differences, but for now understand that Alzheimer's is a form of dementia. The end result for all dementias is the same."

With that, his irritated nurse who had been consistently looking at her watch whisked Dr. Zimmer from the room, and on they went to his next patient.

Back home, I started my computer research on dementia and its many forms. I read with dread each new article. The devastating knowledge that I now could not fix Mom crushed me. My dream of helping Mom and enjoying her company was slowly being destroyed.

Overwhelmed, I turned to Rocky. On a daily basis she had been my confidante and sage. Angry or frustrated with Mom, I would call Rocky crying. No matter what she was doing, she stopped and took the time to listen. After this initial appointment with Dr. Zimmer, Rocky, hearing the desperation in my voice, decided it was time to make a trip up north. She wanted to meet Dr. Cee on his next home visit, when he would give Mom the conclusion of the doctors' combined diagnoses.

We both knew we were now on a life-altering journey.

With guidance from Dr. Cee we determined it was best for him to tell Mom the truth about her condition. He arrived on one of those summer days that remind me why I live in upstate New York. The sky was bright blue, with light green spring leaves just beginning to turn to their darker summer shades. The temperature and humidity were perfect, allowing me to enjoy the warmth of the sun and the cool breeze, as it brushed the hair from my face. I longed to be outside doing anything other than enduring the scenario that was taking place in my home.

While Rocky and I gently took Mom's hands, Dr. Cee, with his kind eyes and soft voice, gently told Mom she had dementia. It was brutal to watch her expression change from denial to realization. Mom asked a few questions, then became silent and eventually lost interest in what was going on around her.

Rocky and I questioned Dr. Cee as to what we should do next. He set us on a path giving us the tools to gather the necessary information we would need to help Mom in her final years. We were inundated with lists of websites and books to read. It was also suggested we contact our local Alzheimer's association.

Later that evening, Mom did not seem bothered at all by the news she had received and we avoided the topic like the proverbial elephant in the room, believing Mom accepted her fate with ease. Mom's calm reaction became apparent and heartrending upon Dr. Cee's subsequent visits. Each time Mom would ask him the same question. It wasn't that she didn't believe him; the truth was she couldn't remember from visit to visit what he told her. I grieved each time she accepted the news when she would ask in a strong determined voice, "What is wrong with me?"

Dr. Cee would answer every time as gently as he did the first:

"Corki, you have dementia."

## Movie Night

My family was settling into our 24/7 life with Mom and all that came with it, including very little personal time for Paul and me.

We decided we needed a date night. We negotiated with Kristen and came up with an agreement that worked for all of us. She could have her boyfriend over for dinner with us then she would be in charge of Grammy Cork. Kristen decided the evening wouldn't be a total loss because, over the years, she and her grandmother always enjoyed watching Harry Potter movies together and she looked forward to continuing that tradition.

We explained to Mom that Paul and I were going out and Kristen's boyfriend would be leaving right after supper, giving the two of them the night together. We headed out with confidence of a plan well executed. According to Kristen, as soon as the door to the house closed, Mom returned to her days when the girls were very young and she my dad would babysit when visiting. Mom knew she was the adult; she did not remember, though, or acknowledge that Kristen was seventeen and no longer needed to be taken care of. Kristen said good-bye to her boyfriend who exited our home through the garage and walked back into the family room.

"Grammy, what do you want to do now? Should we watch a movie?"

"Kristen, I know what you are up to. I saw your boyfriend go into the garage. I know that he is waiting out there for you. I know he lives out there and you are planning on joining him."

"No, Grammy, he went to his car in the driveway and drove home."

"Kristen, I wasn't born yesterday. I am going to stay down here and keep an eye on that door."

"Grammy, let's just watch a movie, it will be fun."

"No, I am watching you."

With reluctance, Kristen went upstairs to her bedroom. The craziness did not stop there.

Mom became concerned that Kristen had escaped. She called Kristen back downstairs. Once Mom was satisfied Kristen was in the house she then began to fret the boyfriend was, too. Mom proceeded to hunt through each room in the house, not an easy task for a woman in her physical condition. As Mom searched, she stumbled with her cane and wheezed with the exertion turning on lights everywhere she went.

Finally, content the boyfriend was not in the house, she made Kristen return to her room. She tried to follow Kristen up the stairs, but struggled so Kristen had to help her. As Mom weaved on her unsteady legs into her bedroom, she warned, "Kristen, I am going to be in my room, I will be able to see you if you leave your room."

"Grammy, I'm not going anywhere."

"Well, I'll be watching."

And she did. When Kristen started down the stairs an hour later for a snack, Mom yelled at her. If she had to go to the bathroom, Mom stood guard.

We came home after a wonderful night out. Paul and I were startled as we drove up to our house to find it lit up like a prison yard. We gave each other the same bewildered look.

Upon entering the house, we were surprised to find Mom awake sitting up in bed, long past her normal bedtime.

"Hey, Mom, what is the problem? Why are you still awake?"

"Kristen was trying to leave with her boyfriend."

Feeling confused, I turned to Kristen as she came barging out of her room like an animal released from a cage.

"Mom, it was nuts here. Grammy thinks my boyfriend lives in the garage and she wouldn't let me out of my room all night."

As Kristen stomped down the stairs, she yelled over her shoulder, "I'm starving and I am going downstairs for a snack."

It took me awhile to calm Mom down and convince her I would take care of the boyfriend. The damage to Kristen's relationship with her grandmother was done. I knew the grandmother Kristen had grown up loving, her fierce, independent, thoughtful, competitive game-playing Grammy Cork, was no longer alive for Kristen.

**Lighten Up**

Tempers were short and laughter was hard to find, as most days it was difficult to persuade Mom to do anything other than sit in her favorite wingback chair in the family room, either watching TV or reading a book. One day she broke the silence. I observed Mom staring intently at our small cherry tree planted just outside the arched window.

Eventually she asked, "What kind of bird is that in the tree?"

I was busy cleaning up the lunch mess so I looked up briefly and not seeing a bird, I replied, "I don't see anything Mom, it must have flown away."

"No, it is right there in the tree."

I walked closer and still saw nothing. Puzzled, I asked, "Do you mean the leaves moving with the breeze?"

"No, it's a bird right in front of you."

"Hmm, not sure, Mom. I can't tell what kind of bird that is," I lied. Back in the kitchen, I attributed Mom's mistaken sighting to her fading vision and mentally added a visit to the eye doctor to my To Do list.

The next day we had a similar conversation. Once again, I walked over to the tree and searched it seeing only branches and leaves. Mom was insistent. I questioned her once again. "What does it look like, Mom? What color is it?"

"It's brown."

Mom's bird sighting continued for several days. She asked each family member in turn to tell her what kind of bird was in the tree. She was relentless and would not be silenced with causal remarks of how the bird must have flown off. It was maddening for all of us. We wanted to prove to Mom that there was no bird.

My nephew, Michael, Mom's oldest grandson, was coming for a visit. As the weekend approached, the thought of his stay brightened everyone's attitude with the knowledge it would break the monotony of our caretaking. Our stomachs growled with the anticipation of Michael cooking our favorite Italian recipe we fondly call "Michael's Sauce." He pulled into the drive after his long journey up the east coast from Washington D.C., and with enthusiasm, he burst into the family room. As he settled onto the couch to begin his initial conversation, Mom immediately interrupted with her queries about the bird. We were intent on hearing Michael's stories, so we tried to ignore her politely. Mom's repeated question became louder and more insistent. Paul's frustration climaxed. Suddenly, in mid conversation, Paul ran out the door to the cherry tree. We watched with alarm as he began to frantically grab leaves, shake branches violently, while screaming through the open window, "Is *this* the bird, Corki?"

Paul continued repeating the question as the rest of us sat there stunned. Wanting to prove once and for all to Mom there was no damn bird, if there actually had ever been a bird in the cherry tree it was long gone with all of the commotion.

Michael looked around at our intense faces; he watched as Paul practically pulled the tree up by its roots. Michael was unaware this had been an ongoing conversation for days and was shocked by my typically composed husband and his apparent overreaction to a simple question. It was obvious to the rest of us that Paul was taking his aggravation of the past few months out on this small tree. So much so that we all began to echo Paul's claim that, indeed, there was no bird to be found.

Michael began to laugh at all of us. "Whoa, you guys need to lighten up around here. You are taking everything way too seriously."

Our irrational exclamations and wild gestures were halted abruptly with Michael's remark. We recognized our appearance was comical to someone not familiar with the adjustments my family was forced to make. We began to laugh at ourselves. Our laughter turned to guffaws as we released the frustration of coming to terms with Mom and her dementia and its impact on our family. Combined with our laughter was the realization that we all needed to relinquish control of what the future would bring. With this release, came the understanding that humor was a much needed ingredient to our household mix and that we would require plenty of it as we continued our care of Mom.

Eventually, we discovered that Mom was hallucinating which is common with her form of dementia. If she watched the news and they talked about al-Qaeda, suddenly armed men in long robes would appear on our back deck. Another time she spotted a car full of teenagers in our backyard as they drove across the lawn. She saw babies everywhere and the bird continued to make an occasional appearance.

As determined on the day of Michael's visit, we used humor whenever possible to overcome the frustration and sadness that enveloped our lives.

**Rocky Steps In**

Trying to maintain a regular family life with Mom's additional needs continued to fray my nerves. She had been living with us since the beginning of May; it was now late in the summer and I needed a break. Rocky, hearing the stress in my voice, took control. During one of our frequent phone conversations, she stated with authority, "I am coming to visit. You and Paul need to plan a getaway for the weekend."

Paul and I followed orders and made our arrangements. As any responsible caretaker would do, I left detailed instructions much as a mother would when leaving a small child with a babysitter. Paul, wanting to help, drew maps to local restaurants, shopping malls and pointed out several nearby grocery stores. Rocky chased us out the door assuring us all would go smoothly.

"Don't worry, we'll be fine," Rocky admonished jokingly. "Besides, I have Catlin to help."

Of course, Rocky was right. Catlin was home for the summer from college and knew the ins and outs of caring for her grandmother. I realized with a sigh of relief that Rocky was more than capable and Catlin was a good advisor. Together they could handle Mom's care for the weekend.

As we rounded the corner out of our neighborhood, Paul and I chuckled over how quickly we jumped into our car to make our escape. In an effort to ignore our worries, we decided not to call home. If a problem arose, Rocky or Catlin would contact us. We headed north into the Adirondacks, a place that always brought us peace.

Tranquility was not the order of the day, unfortunately, back home with Mom.

Mom became upset when she realized I had left and would not return for a couple of days. She sensed Rocky's inexperience and felt vulnerable. Almost immediately, she began to advise Rocky.

"Posey usually serves dinner around six. We watch *The Daily Show* at seven."

"No problem, Mom. Posey wrote everything down for me."

"Did she tell you I go to bed at ten?"

Rocky chuckled to herself. I had explained that Mom fought me on the ten o'clock bedtime but Mom, wanting to stick to her routine, made no mention that they might want to stay up later.

Instead of watching TV while dinner cooked, Mom came into the kitchen to make sure Rocky knew what she was doing. She questioned the ingredients and Rocky's technique, causing her to feel inadequate.

"Well, Posey does it differently."

"I know, Mom, but I think you will like this recipe anyway."

Despite Mom's interrogations, Rocky managed to put dinner on the table. She relaxed slightly as Catlin and a skeptical Mom settled in to enjoy the meal.

Rocky was learning with each passing hour just how difficult Mom's care truly was. Bedtime was another escapade. Rocky tried to follow my instructions, but by evening Mom was suffering from the sun downing effect. It is a common occurrence with dementia patients; they become confused and unsettled as evening approaches. Mom sensed her normal routine was not the same. Consequently, she questioned and argued with Rocky on every move, and Mom's normal bedtime ritual stretched well past the customary half hour. Once Mom was safely in bed, Rocky slipped downstairs for a drink and some alone time. Feeling frustrated and incompetent she contemplated calling us, but decided to persevere in her weekend duties and not bother us.

The next morning, Catlin and Rocky felt they needed to get out of the house and take Mom on an outing. Together they determined they could do this! "Your Mom does it by herself all the time, and there are two of us."

After a breakfast conversation that lingered over several cups of coffee, Rocky decided they had waited long enough and went upstairs to wake Mom. She soon discovered the lack of enthusiasm Mom had for mornings. This, coupled with Mom's alarm at not seeing my face walk through her bedroom door, caused a major delay in the plan. It took Rocky an hour to coax Mom from bed. When she finally sat up, Mom announced, she had to have coffee before getting dressed, so down the stairs they went with Mom still in her robe. She lingered over her coffee and, when finished, announced she was hungry. This was unusual for Mom; she never ate breakfast. Looking at the clock, Catlin and Rocky decided they should just have lunch before their excursion.

Mom still needed to get dressed, which was always a lengthy process. Rocky laid out Mom's outfit, per my instructions, as it was confusing for Mom to make decisions. In my notes, I also added: don't wander too far away, Mom may call for help, and get her toiletries ready while she dresses.

*Easy enough*, Rocky thought. After what seemed like eternity, Mom moved from her bedroom to the bathroom and eventually proclaimed she was ready. Catlin grabbed Mom's jacket and she quickly bundled her into it. Together they hustled her into the car, strapped on the seatbelt and headed to the mall.

After only a few minutes, Mom proclaimed she was tired. Rocky, preoccupied with shopping said, "OK, Mom, just sit in this comfy chair for a few minutes while Catlin and I finish looking around." They secured Mom and walked a few aisles over to look at shoes.

A short few minutes later, over the loud speaker they heard: "Will Ruthanna Christle please come to the customer service desk?"

Rocky and Catlin looked at each other. Startled like a train barreling down on them, they realized immediately they had become distracted and lost track of Mom. Rocky barked, "You go look for Grammom; I'll go to the customer service desk."

Catlin scurried away and located her grandmother looking at clothing not far from the chair from which she had wandered. Rocky was pleased to discover that an honest person had found Mom's purse where she had left it, on the now empty chair. Stressed, the pair came to the conclusion that shopping was no longer a good option; they decided it was time for an early dinner at a small Italian restaurant. Once seated at their table Catlin helped her Grammom take off her jacket. It was then Rocky discovered that Mom had not worn the pretty shirt she had laid out, but a dirty sweatshirt and she had forgotten to wear a bra. Of less consequence was the fact Mom did not have on her make-up.

When the food arrived, Mom complained, "I can't chew this."

Rocky looked up and to her horror realized Mom did not have her teeth in. Falling back and sliding down in her chair in defeat, Rocky laughed at herself and thought; *In one afternoon I have managed to get Mom out of the house hours behind schedule, dressed in dirty clothing, without a bra, no make-up and no teeth. While shopping, I lost her and her purse in a store. Obviously, this is much more difficult than it looks. Posey makes it look so easy.*

Mom and Rocky
2007

Rocky and me in our
Purdue comfort clothes
2008

Rocky and me with Mom in temporary
nursing home
late October 2009

## Coming To Terms

My relationship with Mom continued to deteriorate. She had become the whiny child who argued about everything and I had become a frustrated parent. The uncomfortable situation of Mom living with me, my guilt at realizing it wasn't working and that I couldn't fix it, became very clear with a simple statement from Kristen. After helping her grandmother up the stairs, walking behind to keep her from falling, she came back into the family room and sat beside me.

"Mom, you have got to convince Grammy Corki to take a shower. She reeks."

The statement was said without malice, yet it stung me to the core. With Kristen's words I had to admit and accept the fact, I could no longer care for Mom in our home.

This realization had been forming in my brain and heart for quite some time. I recalled the hundreds of instances Mom and I argued over her hygiene, even though she was down to bathing only once a week. Getting Mom up and moving took much of the morning. The evening ritual lasted just as long but as I was exhausted and emotionally drained, the task seemed more daunting. She no longer participated in our household; instead, Mom would sit hours on end in the family room flipping through the television channels with the volume at ear piercing decibels. Yet, if we wandered out of her sight, she would panic. With each passing day, another sign of her progressing dementia would become apparent. I realized that Mom was only comfortable in our family room. She no longer wandered through the remainder of our home. Because of this Mom now refused to leave the house with me so I had to wait for a family member to relieve me so I could run errands. We tried hiring aides to watch Mom, but they were unreliable. On many days, I would make plans only to get a call that morning saying the aide couldn't make it.

Due to these unrelenting demands, I began to panic. Even though it was late summer, the dream of Mom staying at our ski house and reading books or of her traveling with us to Kristen's ski races was no longer

166

feasible. *What will I do all winter?* I was miserable at the thought of missing travel with Kristen, her team, and the other families during her last year in high school. It broke my heart.

When all seemed lost, when every decision seemed impossible to make, I once again called my go-to sister, Rocky. She listened and consoled as I poured my heart out. Rocky said she would think about our family dilemma. Then, with the enlisted help of my sister Rhonda in Oregon, the two of them began to talk me into finding a new place for Mom to live. They called and sent emails daily. They encouraged me by expressing how proud they were of me. They repeatedly said:

> You saved Mom's life by bringing her to
> your home. You nursed her back to health,
> organized her medications, and made her
> feel loved. Now you must consider yourself,
> your husband, and your children. Think
> about what is best for all of you *and* Mom.
> It is time for her to move from your home.

I struggled with envisioning Mom anywhere other than the safety of our home. To complicate matters, Mom panicked at the mention of assisted living, believing it would be a nursing home, her worst nightmare.

With my sisters' encouragement, I finally gave up my hope of fixing Mom. I allowed my heart to adjust to the logic of Rhonda and Rocky's reasoning. Once again, Rocky made the flight north from Atlanta and together we began the daunting task of finding Mom a new place to live.

Paul suggested I contact the Alzheimer's Association. Their response was amazing. Within a few short days, I had an appointment with a counselor at a local restaurant. Paul and I went together, before Rocky had a chance to fly in. We told her our dilemma, our concerns, our inability to know where to begin. She listened, asked questions and suggested a course of action. She gave us several brochures so we could learn about places in the area that accepted dementia patients.

Relieved, I set up meetings and tours for the three days Rocky would be in town, based on the outline presented by our dementia counselor.

Rocky works well under pressure and is an excellent planner. She brought with her the book *The 36 Hour Day* by Nancy L. Mace M.A. and Peter V. Rabins M.D., M.P.H. This book was a great reference for us; it became our bible. We gleaned from its pages the information we needed to critically analyze the homes we would tour. We also formed a list of questions we should ask. I drove while Rocky read excerpts from the book and jotted down notes. We were an amazing and enthusiastic team.

The first place we visited came highly recommended. We approached the high-rise building with trepidation; Mom would not like living so high up. We met the director and entered the elevator. As the doors slid open, we were assaulted with a smell we associated only with hospitals. Directly in front of us was a bustling nurses' station. We saw several patients sitting throughout the hallways or in the game room, a barren space with tile floors, small windows and a blaring TV. Many of the residents sat in wheelchairs, some bent over in sleep. There were no private rooms and a flimsy curtain separated the beds. It made us both shudder; we could not leave the facility fast enough. As we exited, we saw a garbage can. With finality, we threw the information packet in as we rushed to our car.

Day One:  Depressing as hell.

We hoped Day Two would be better.

The subsequent facilities we visited were much nicer. We found private rooms, quiet places to sit, and other spaces designated for TV viewing. There were activities for the residents. Yet, something did not click with us; we still got the feeling of a "facility," not a "home." Afterwards, going over our notes and thoughts, we realized in the different buildings we observed there were courtyards, but the areas weren't available full time to the residents as the entrance doors were locked. We smiled at the residents, but they did not respond. Instead, they stared at nothing with vacant eyes. We also felt something missing when the directors discussed their residents. We felt they lacked compassion, and fondness for those left in their care. It also seemed to us families were not truly encouraged to participate in any daily activities. One director went so far as to scold us for not being better prepared with all of the medical information she would need to admit our mother. Although admitting residents to her facility was routine to her, she did not seem to take into account this move was new and frightening to us. We wanted a place that cared and respected our mother *and* her family. Rocky and I headed home to dinner and several glasses of wine to purge our disappointment.

On our final day, we woke with dread that we would never complete our goal. We had one last scheduled appointment. Here, with relief, we met with an enthusiastic admissions coordinator. She walked us through a unique place which she was quick to point out was not a facility, but a "community."

"This is home to our residents and we treat it as such," She said with pride.

She guided us through a lovely one-story building. Each resident had their own room; the hallways completed a circle so that wandering residents did not get lost. The kitchen was in the center of the house, with the family room on one side and dining tables on the other. We viewed and admired inner courtyards that were open all the time brimming with fragrant, colorful gardens, and we observed residents sitting in patio chairs sipping drinks. We immediately recognized the respect the caretakers showed for the residents. There was a feeling of home, comfort. We fell in love. Glancing at Rocky, I knew she felt the same way I did.

We told our admissions coordinator we pictured our mother being happy living there. She cringed and said, "There is just one problem. We do not have an opening right now."

Our hearts dropped, but were lifted in the next moment when she mentioned their newly built community that was just beginning to admit residents. This home was further away, but it didn't matter - we wanted to see it. The glitch was that Rocky was leaving the following afternoon. Our admissions coordinator agreed to give us a tour the next morning, her day off, as long as she could bring her daughter who loved visiting the residents. That evening at dinner we both asked God to give us a sign as this was a difficult decision and we had to be sure.

The following morning we timed the drive to East Greenbush from my home in Clifton Park. It took us less than thirty minutes. I decided that was doable. Rocky and I walked into Hawthorne Ridge Community, both knowing this was our last hope. We stood close to each other for comfort and support. Smiling faces, beautiful decorations, and warm-colored walls and carpets greeted us. Inside we found a family room with a TV, a smaller living room with a fireplace, and a large kitchen with several tables and chairs for the residents. We met an aide who cried when she told us how she loved working here; it was her calling after her mom passed away from Alzheimer's.  Rocky and I once again glanced at each other and confirmed with a nod; this looked promising.

"If we were to move our mother here, what would her room look like?"

"Since she would be one of our first residents, you can pick her room. In the back hall are the rooms with the best view. I will show you those first."

We walked into a corner room. It was big and had an adjoining private bath, as did all of the rooms. She brought us further down the hall and we poked our heads in the doorway of another room. Through the window, we saw the most gorgeous view, a hill of trees climbing into a bright blue sky. We gasped. Since moving to upstate New York Mom always commented on how much she enjoyed our abundant, beautiful trees over the vacant farm fields of Indiana.

This was our sign. Both Rocky and I began to cry.

Extended Family portrait
2008

Mom and Four generations
on Lake George in the Adirondacks

Matching outfits for Christmas
Mom with one of her great grandchildren
Christmas 2007

Christmas Day at our home
2007

A Birthday kiss from me on Mom's 85th Birthday
July 2009

Kristen, Catlin, me and Mom
2009

Paul, Mom, me
2009

## Resentment

During the course of Mom's stay at my house, I frequently updated my six siblings by email. The information I shared with them included Mom's current condition including problems with balance and falling, her lack of stamina, diet and medication issues. As the months stole away, other topics of concern were Mom's uncooperative behavior, especially with hygiene, her mounting confusion and finally Mom's diagnosis of dementia.

On more than one occasion, I told my siblings that leaving Mom home alone was not an option. I wrote detailed explanations about the troubles we had bringing aides into our house. I felt I had the support of my siblings with the decision to move Mom from my home to assisted living. Believing this, Rocky cheerfully sent out the following email with my approval. In part, the email described our efforts to locate a new home for Mom and how excited we were with our discovery.

Tuesday, September 11, 2007

...Do you believe in signs??? Posey and I
have always joked about having signs really
visible because we sometimes can't figure
them out. When we walked into Hawthorne
Ridge we knew we had found a home for
Mom!... It is a brand new facility. The last
wing will open this week. As we walked the
halls meeting residents we liked what we
saw. The place was bright with many
windows, off-white walls with bright green
and blue chairs with a little red in them.
Very cheery looking. Country kitchens
where you gather to eat. One wing the
residents changed part of the eating area to
include couches to watch TV together. We
met Colleen who was on staff that day. She
just got back from vacation and fought back
tears saying how much she missed her

family at Hawthorne. Her job was her purpose!...

The sign that made us cry was when we walked into a room to discover the beautiful hillside full of trees. Mom's dream of seeing the leaves change will come true. We just can't believe how blessed we are to have found such a place for Mom to live. The residents in this area all have some form of dementia. The director allowed us to walk the new wing to choose the best room for Mom. Everything is brand new! Mom will be the first to live in her room. We chose the room with the beautiful hillside with trees out two windows (one in bathroom). Her door to her room faces the courtyard as well. Right around her room is a small sitting area. We thought this would motivate Mom to do some interacting.

Choosing a facility was one of the most difficult things Posey and I have ever done.

Yes, we did break down several times. We had been so stressed about it and wanted to have a solution where Mom could live with her dementia. We feel this is a blessing that we have found this home for Mom. We appreciate all your positive thoughts and prayers you sent with us. We thank you for being there in spirit with us.


Love,
Rocky


The joy and gratefulness Rocky and I felt about finding Mom the perfect place to live did not last long. We were crushed with the negative responses from our siblings. Big families are challenging; everyone has an opinion. Beneath the outward appearances are the underlying, family dynamics. Who got what as children? Who feels robbed? Did some children receive more love than others? How about monetary support? Were our parents more generous with some than others? Older children feel they should lead; younger children do not feel so young anymore and want to express  opinions. Questions began to pour in. Most said that Rocky and I were rushing the decision about where Mom should be living. More than one sibling wanted to know if we had considered hiring full time help for Mom in her home in Wabash, and had we not considered the assisted living community back home. Some siblings thought perhaps we were jumping the gun and Mom would regain her health enough to live on her own.

Rocky and I were shocked. How could these suggestions come up now? In the years since our father had passed away, what did some of our siblings think Rocky and I were doing with our visits to Mom? Had they missed our communication describing how we had taken Mom on a tour of the assisted living community near her home? Did they overlook the fact we had hired, and then Mom promptly fired, live-in help at her home? How could they forget when Mom lived alone Rocky and I arranged for a Medical-Call necklace that she refused to use? But, more than that, we were baffled with their reactions, especially based on descriptions I was giving about Mom's health, and her physical and mental well being. Were my siblings in such denial that they could not comprehend the information I sent them several times a week? My breaking point came when my brother, Tim, suggested the only reason Mom was moving out of my house was so that I could go skiing every weekend.

Phone calls began to go back and forth consisting of hurtful arguments and hang-ups on both ends. Many mornings I would open my email to cruel notes accusing me of trying to force Mom into a move she did not need. After several days of nasty and hurtful messages, I broke into hot, gushing tears. The sobs became uncontrollable. My emotional breakdown related to my self-induced guilt because I was not able to "fix" Mom and the stress I felt trying to maintain some normalcy in our family life. These two factors, combined with my realization that my siblings were questioning my care of our Mom and accusing me of evil motives, sent me over the edge of self-control.

A rift began to form among Mom's seven children. I had always thought we were a typical family. Even though we lived scattered across the United States, we visited each other when possible, celebrating birthdays and sister vacations. Of course, we had our disagreements and ups and downs, but until now we had managed.

Despite all this, Rocky and I moved forward with our plan to move Mom to Hawthorne Ridge. The emotions from all sides calmed to a simmer. Our sibling relationships limped along for several months encumbered with an underlying current of hurt running throughout the family.

## Moving Day

No matter how we tried to approach it, October 11, 2007, began and ended badly. On that day, Rocky and I moved our mother to Hawthorne Ridge.

Three days prior to the move Rocky and I had diligently worked to prepare Mom's new living space. Looking through her huge windows, we watched as the leaves on the trees began to turn and seem to burn with the colors of fall. Hawthorne Ridge's dementia unit consisted of three homes, connected via hallways. Each home contained sixteen bedrooms with private baths a large, inviting kitchen and adjoining living room along with several common areas to enjoy. There was also a sizable community space for all three houses to gather in.

Rocky and I approached the matter of décor for Mom's room as one would when moving a child into a college dorm. Knowing Mom loved the color red, we started with our inspiration piece: a small night-light that had a burgundy lampshade with small beads dangling from it. We were anxious to create a room that would take our mother's breath away when she entered. Since Mom did not really have any pieces from her home that would work in this small space, we purchased new. Sticking with our theme, we found burgundy curtains and a complementing taupe bedspread with black designs across it. We purchased Mom's favorite kind of chair, a recliner and acquired a small black distressed nightstand and a matching cupboard for her linens. Pictures of Mom and Dad were hung and additional pictures of her children and grandchildren lined a high shelf that circled the room.

Rocky and I felt good about our design choices as the room brightened with each accessory we added.

The staff told us it was often better not to tell your loved one they were moving until that morning, or at least the night before. Consequently, Rocky and I slipped out several mornings before Mom awoke to do our shopping. Our goal each day was to return before Mom got out of bed. Complications arose when Mom woke up earlier than expected.

"Where have you girls been?" She inquired suspiciously. We felt like high school teenagers who had just been caught staying out past curfew.

"Mom, we had some errands to run and Posey needed to buy some things to mail to Catlin." Rocky lied, convincingly.

"Well, I don't know, it seems you girls are up to something." Rocky rolled her eyes at me and I walked from the room before more questions could be asked.

After several days of fast-paced, extensive shopping followed by an afternoon of frantic decorating, Mom's moving in day loomed before us. Heeding the staff's experienced advice Rocky and I felt we had to admit to Mom the truth.

The evening before the move, we sat with Mom and held her hands as Rocky gently said, "Mom, you have mentioned on more than one occasion, that you are worried about the burden you are putting on Posey and her family. They, in turn, have honestly replied, they asked you to live with them because they felt it was a good move for everyone. But, things have changed. The physical work of helping you bathe and dress and move from one floor to another in Posey's house is becoming too difficult."

Tears filled our eyes as we saw Mom's face acknowledge the reality of the words.

I added, "Mom, I think you know that getting up and down my stairs is a struggle. And, I am having a hard time helping you with your daily care. So, Rocky and I, along with most of your children, have agreed that a move to an assisted living community is the best option for all of us."

"Well, I think we are doing fine." Mom retorted.

"Mom, you argue with me about bathing, you say you are lonely for people your own age. You don't really participate with my family anymore. And you hate to be alone. This new place will have lots of people for you to talk with, play games with, and watch TV with. You will have people your own age to eat meals with. The staff will help you with bathing and dressing."

I watched as she realized she no longer wanted to own the complaints she had been voicing for weeks. I could tell our idea appealed to her, but she still was adamant about not moving. I also knew, Mom's biggest fear was thinking she was going to be dumped somewhere and left without any family to visit her.

"I will come and visit you several times a week, Mom. I will still take you to all of your doctor appointments, hair and nail appointments. We can even go out for lunch."

Mom replied arrogantly, "It seems you girls have already made up your minds so I guess I don't have much choice."

That was the extent of our conversation. We did not speak of the move again; in fact, few words were spoken that night. Rocky and I shared some Bushmill's Irish Whiskey, a tradition that was started some years before among our siblings based on our Irish heritage. We acknowledged with glances and a silent toast to each other that bringing Mom to Hawthorne Ridge was going to make for a very long day.

No one slept well that night. Rising early, Rocky and I showered and drank too much coffee while we regrouped. We stuck with our decision to wake Mom at 9:00 a.m. If all went well we could have her dressed, fed and out the door by 10:30. We had an 11:00 o'clock appointment at Hawthorne Ridge to sign papers and we wanted to get Mom situated in her new room before lunch. We spent the previous afternoon putting the final touches on decorating her room. It was standing ready for her initial viewing.

Rocky and I walked up the stairs to Mom's bedroom. Stressed, I felt my stomach flip-flop and I wished I hadn't had that second cup of coffee. Together, we opened the door to her room and found Mom lying on her back snoring. The room was filled with morning light and the birds in the trees were visible through the windows. I approached her bed and, with a slight tap on her shoulder, tried to wake her.

"Mom, it's another beautiful day, time to get up. Rocky and I have coffee made." Her eyes fluttered as she struggled to wake up.

"I don't want to get up now. I didn't get any sleep last night and I am tired. I'll get up later."

"But Mom, we have an appointment at eleven so you really need to get up now."

She rolled over, pulled the blankets over her eyes and went back to sleep. Rocky and I had the same exchange with her every few minutes for the next hour. Mom seemed to remember our conversation from the night before. She dreaded the thought of this day. Mom's unwillingness to cooperate made it that much more difficult for us to control our feelings of guilt and question if we were doing the right thing.

Finally, with much coaxing and convincing that the place we were taking her was nothing like her dreaded vision of a nursing home, we got Mom into the car. We were way past our eleven o'clock appointment, but we just had to go with the flow of the day. Paul had offered to help by coming along, but we had decided it would be better if it were just Rocky and me. Now we were beginning to doubt that decision. Perhaps Paul would have been a buffer between mother and daughters. We drove the half hour to Hawthorne Ridge mostly in silence. Rocky and I had run out of things to say and Mom sat frozen with anxiety.

As we got closer I said, "Mom, this is the road you will live on and here is a library you can get books from."

As we approached a YMCA, a large structure with few windows and screens that appeared to be bars, Mom exclaimed, "I knew it. You girls are taking me to a home."

"What? No. Mom, that is not where you will live. Here is you new home."

As we rounded the final curve, the lovely green and brown buildings of the Hawthorne Ridge community came into view.

"Mom, your home is here in these buildings."

Pulling to a stop under the covered entrance Rocky and I helped Mom from the car. She was visibly upset and I didn't blame her, but we had to keep moving. I jumped back into the car to park it as Rocky helped Mom inside. Catching up to them, we stopped and said hello at the front desk to the receptionist Rocky and I had become friendly with. After proceeding down a long hallway filled with tall sunlight windows, we reached the locked door. I punched it the pass code.

"Why is the door locked?"

"That is for security, to protect the residents so no one who isn't supposed to be here can get in."

Mom liked this explanation. With her dementia, Mom had developed a new fear of people breaking in. Several members of the staff greeted us as we wound our way to Mom's room. The woman I was supposed to meet to sign the paperwork stopped us. As I apologized for being behind schedule, she smiled and said that she understood.

"See Mom, everyone is friendly and isn't this place lovely?"

I pointed out the décor as I said. "I love these colors and decorations and there are so many windows. Look, this one has a view out onto a courtyard with beautiful gardens."

We passed the kitchen and living room where the other residents were gathered watching TV. Finally, we approached Mom's room pointing out the small display case next to the door.

"See Mom, there is your name and Rocky put pictures of you so that others will know who you are."

We did not receive any comment from her. Mom was intent on letting us verbally trip all over ourselves. We opened the door and Mom spotted her new recliner. "Is that mine?"

"Yes, we bought it for you."

"I would like to sit in it. I'm tired."

She hobbled over to the chair and with our help slid into the seat. I raised the footrest and Mom began to look around and acknowledged our work without a smile. We sat in silence letting her soak it all in. Eventually, we pointed out the attributes of her room and she listened, but did not comment.

"Mom, look out this big window, you have a hill of trees to watch as they turn to their pretty fall colors. And, see all of your pictures. You have your own bathroom and this is the new bedspread we bought you. Everything in this room belongs to you."

A staff member dropped in and welcomed us to join them at dinner.

"Mom, are you hungry? I know I am."

"No, I'm not hungry. I'm too upset."

"Well, let's just walk to the kitchen. I'm sure they would at least give you a cup of coffee."

Rocky and I began to wean Mom from us and introduce her to the staff. They were very friendly. The three of us were presented with bowls of soup and salads. Rocky and I enjoyed the meal. Mom picked at hers refusing eat. Rocky and I chatted with the other residents and the staff while Mom sat rigidly in her chair, not looking at anyone. The icebreaker came when Mom was served dessert, her favorite part of any meal. Mom began to relax as the delicious sweets settled into her stomach. Her preconceived notions of a nursing home were quickly dissolving, but I knew it would take Mom awhile longer to accept she could be happy here. After dinner, we returned to Mom's room. Throughout the late evening and into the early night staff members wandered in and introduced themselves. "Corki, we are here for you. If you need anything you just pull this cord and we will come running."

Rocky and I stayed until dark. We helped Mom change into her nightgown and tucked her into bed. Mom was exhausted, as were Rocky and I. She clung to her blankets like a small child and my heart broke to leave her there alone, she seemed so frightened. But eventually, we said one last good-bye and turned off the lights, leaving her new nightlight burning. We stood outside her room for several minutes, but we did not hear Mom call for anything. My eyes burned with fatigue and sorrow, a lump formed in my throat. Rocky and I walked the hallways in silence, trying to keep our tears at bay. But once in the car, we cried all the way home.

Thinking the worst was behind us. Rocky and I could not have fathomed what would occur in the coming months.

## The Final Break

Mom had been living at Hawthorne Ridge for more than half a year. She was settled in and, when asked, said she enjoyed living there. She liked the people and the routine. I took pleasure in the fact we had re-established more of a mother daughter relationship since I was no longer her main caregiver. When we went to get her nails done, we often stopped at our favorite diner for lunch. If we went to a doctor's appointment, we stopped for dessert afterwards. It was a lot of work on my part. Since Mom couldn't walk far, I would drop her off at the entrance, find a place to safely leave her, then run and park the car. Getting her in and out of the car was difficult because I had to help her step up to the seat and then manage the seatbelt. As time went on, Mom remembered less about how to get in and out of the car so I would have to talk her through it and then do a lot of pulling and pushing to get her situated. She still enjoyed our outings so it was always worth the effort.

Mom had done a good job of keeping her affairs in order while living in Indiana. After my father passed away, she rewrote her will and tied up loose ends. Once Mom moved in with me, I wanted to keep all legal issues transparent for the benefit of my siblings. I hired an elder care attorney for Mom.

Mom's new attorney highly recommended to me, due to Mom's dementia, that I be granted Mom's Power of Attorney. The attorney suggested we include another sibling, but I was the only one living in New York and we agreed it would be too difficult to pursue that avenue. Also, under the advice of Mom's lawyer, we moved her money and investment portfolio to a financial advisor in state. This made transactions and tracking Mom's finances easier for me. Because of questions already surfacing from some of my siblings, I sent them the financial advisor's name and told them to contact him with any questions. It was he who suggested that holding onto her house and two cars was costing money and in order to preserve her finances, it would be best to sell them all.

Although I took his recommendation into consideration, I did not act immediately.

As the harsh but beautiful New York winter was turning into a vibrant green spring, it occurred to me that Mom's house in Indiana had now stood empty for over a year. It was time for me to finally take action and follow the financial advisors professional counsel.

Reluctantly, I sent out the following email on March 26, 2008:

Dear All,

This may be a difficult email to read but one that I feel needs to be sent to keep all informed. After talking with a financial advisor it has been determined that the best thing for Mom's estate is to sell both of her cars and her house. She does not need the money to live but as you can guess these items are pulling money from her estate and she will not need them in the future. The good news is Tim has expressed interest in buying Mom's house and we are in the process of getting an appraisal...

Whether Tim buys the house or not it will need to be cleaned out to prepare it for the market in spring. This is a huge task as all of you can imagine... My plan is to fly in to Wabash on April 28th and spend a week cleaning the house to prepare it for the market. Rocky is planning on joining me to help with this large task. Here is where we need your help. As you all know several items have been designated to each of us in Mom's will. We realize, however, that there may be items that you have given to Mom or Dad that would have sentimental value to you and no one else. Our plan of attack is to try and place these items (such as your family photos sent to Mom and Dad) in a box for you and store them until you can arrange to have them sent to you.

Items that I feel are family treasures will also be stored, and upon Mom's death, will be divided among us. The furniture and other items in the house will be appraised for value...

Of course, I am sure you all remember that some years ago Mom had us each write a list of items we would like to receive from her upon her death. In keeping with her wishes, I will not include these items in the sale.

I understand this note is probably very difficult for you to read but we need to perform these items of business that can also become very personal. Please do not question Mom on decisions that she made years ago. She will only become confused and I am sure it will upset her. Also, I have not discussed with Mom yet that her estate will need to sell her house and cars. I am waiting until all decisions have been made so that the information will be cut and dry and she will not need to worry about what will happen only that things have been taken care of for her...

Thank you for keeping in mind Mom's feelings and letting me handle the discussions with her. Although Mom is doing quite well, especially compared to a year ago, she still has trouble remembering recent events. Just last night she once again asked Dr. Cee if she would ever get better so she could go home. Mom cannot remember that she has been diagnosed with dementia and can never live alone...She asks him this every time he visits and it rips my heart out each time. Each visit with the doctor is reliving the experience of Mom learning of such a difficult diagnosis.

Love,

Posey

This email took a simmering family rift and widened it into a gorge.

I thought that if I stated the facts, my siblings would understand the financial issues involved and agree with me. I knew this was an emotional issue, but I could not begin to comprehend the waterfall of rushing arguments that came my way.

My oldest sister, Ranelle, offered the following idea via the first of many emails:

Friday April 11, 2008

Dear Family,

I had an epiphany this morning when I awoke. I believe it is a result of the praying that I did last night...

The thought that came to me is that I can take care of Mom. I can retire from teaching July 09. I had planned to take my retirement and work part time. I can actually be rehired by the school system with benefits and a salary that when added to my teacher retirement keeps me at my current income. I need a few more years paying into Social Security to retire with them.

My plan would include the estate paying me a management salary to take care of Mom... When I thought about it this morning it seemed so clear that my house... would work. We could also spend part of the year at Mom's house in Indiana. I know this will be a big undertaking but feel I can do this. I believe it is the right thing to do...I know this will come as a shock to many of you. Please have an open mind and heart as you consider this plan.

Love,

Ranelle

Several of my siblings agreed this was a wonderful idea. I read the email a number of times to get over my astonishment. Ranelle was suggesting a living arrangement that I had already tried and had proven was too difficult. And, she wanted to get paid for it. On top of that she thought Mom was still capable of living at home and not only that, but moving from one house to the other during the year.

I wondered if Ranelle had read any of *The 36 Hour Day,* the book that Rocky and I affectionately referred to as our bible and had recommended to all our siblings. If so, Ranelle would have learned that dementia patients are happier when their environment remains constant and they prefer small spaces where they can see everything they need. I struggled to understand Ranelle's thinking as it contradicted the information we garnered from the book doctors and from speaking to experts at the Alzheimer's Association.

Incredibly, subsequent emails from my siblings questioned the honesty of both Rocky and I including this one from our sister Robin:

Wednesday April 16, 2008

One reason Ranelle told me why she has brought this care issue up at this time is because Posey has prematurely moved the house decision up. If we look back at the original email, Posey lists that it is just more convenient for her to work on the house now. This is a rather frail reason for leaving Ranelle out of the process...

Mom and Dad had their estate and will set up so that Ranelle, Tim, and...Posey ...work together as a consensus to handle these issues... Hopefully, this group would listen to and consider other family members input in their decision making process and keep all family members informed throughout the steps...Posey had also said in an earlier email that Mom didn't really need the funds from the house at this point so that is not the reason for the schedule change...Of course a simple accounting of the funds would solve this question.

I have now learned that Catlin, and people who she brought with her and who are not related or known to us, were looking through [Mom's] house to find furnishings for {[Catlin's off campus] house at Purdue University.  This situation clearly demonstrates that some oversight is needed. Hence, we need to comply with the three member consensus group.

Thanks,

Robin

*Editor's note: My sister Robin failed to realize that while Mom was alive, I was her only legal financial guardian, through the Power of Attorney. Her confusion lay with the fact that, according to Mom's Will, Ranelle, Tim and I were executors, and decisions for the estate only went into effect after her death.*

Accusations against Rocky and me I could handle, but I did not like my daughter Catlin getting dragged in. Feeling both hurt and enraged I sent the following email.

Wednesday April 16, 2008

As far as cleaning out Mom's house, April is the only time that Rocky and I can get back to Wabash...There seems to be a level of mistrust on the part of Rocky and I cleaning out the house, so let me just state that we are more than happy to relinquish this job to whomever would like to take it over...Please keep in mind that when I picked Mom up last May I did not in any way close down the house. It has stood there vacant for a whole year with every appliance still running, food in the cupboards, if not the refrigerator. These things all need to be taken care of.

It is very apparent to me and several of you that there is no reason to hold onto Mom's house. Yes, I did state Mom does not need the money this year, but how long will it take to sell the house?

I, not Catlin, was going to buy this furniture from the estate. Catlin did meet Tim at Mom's house to see if any of the furniture would be something that I would want to purchase. This opportunity to buy furniture was stated in my original email...However, since this has caused such great concern among some of you, I am no longer interested in purchasing any of the furniture from Mom's estate. Frankly, I am very disappointed in the lack of trust Ranelle and Robin directed towards me...

As stated above, Rocky and I are more than happy to relinquish this job of caring for and cleaning out Mom's house. Please let me know when you intend to take over.

Posey

Not surprisingly, we received no offers of help.

For several days, I awoke to more nasty emails and they often made me cry. One day, my sister Renita called. Hearing my distress over all this unexpected family drama, Renita came to my defense. She told me she would now be in charge of correspondence among siblings. I no longer had to respond to disparaging emails. This allowed me to walk away from the turmoil and stay focused on Mom.

Renita sent out this family email directed at Robin:

Thursday April 24, 2008

...I just called Posey to ask for something... She was sobbing from your letter after spending the day taking care of OUR Mother. Where were you when the original decision [to care for Mom] had to be made that you can act so high and mighty now and demand explanations? Can you lie to yourself and say you didn't know? I knew and didn't act. So did you and everyone else in this family... Rocky and Posey think alike in that they have always come through for Mom and Dad... you kicked them [our parents] out of your house and told them they were not welcome to come back.

We are all going through the emotions of this and no one should be demanding anything at this point unless they want to take over...Asking for a review of accounts is calling someone a thief. I love you and everyone else in my family, but I'm damn tired of people whining and moaning...The estate is not being decided when they clean the house...Do you have the desire to be on call for Mom 24 hours a day? If not, back off! Thank your lucky stars someone else is taking care of it and Mom.

Renita

My sister Rhonda, courageously battling cancer, also came to my defense and sent emails of her own, eloquent, and to the point:

Tuesday July 1, 2008

Dear sisters and brother,

...Love is all that matters. This becomes so apparent to those who are near physical death. Stuff is irrelevant...Losing your Mom is traumatic. Losing your Mom to dementia little by little is almost unbearable. I am grieving every day. I know all of you must be grieving as well even if you aren't aware of it. Posey is faced with this grieving for the loss of Mom and dealing with her care every day. It has to be so difficult for her. That is why it hurts me so much when she doesn't get the full support from her family. Please give her your support in any way you can. I know we all love Mom. I know that Mom loves all of her children...

I know we each see things from our own perspective and perhaps we will never agree. But I believe that yes, Posey should have more say than the rest of us. In fact, I feel that keeping us updated and asking our opinion is not necessary on her part, but her attempt at including everyone. The amount of time that takes is more than she has and the amount of grief she gets in return is outrageous. Sorry, Robin, but she is on the frontline with Mom and doing the work so she gets to have more control...When I call Posey the message I hope to convey and say is "How can I support you? What can I do to help?" That is what each of us should be doing. I don't understand where the lack of trust in Posey comes from? ...It seems to me that there is more concern over the stuff or Mom's house than for the care of Mom. I hope that is a false assumption on my part. But if you read the emails from Ranelle, Tim and Robin, I don't see the concern for Mom; in fact, Mom is rarely mentioned...Posey wants to take care of Mom and I think she is divinely guided.

Posey is the only caregiver in our family. That is just the truth. It doesn't mean that we are less loved by Mom and not good people, we are just not caregivers. It is a matter of personality. As Rocky says, "Posey makes it seem so easy!" Mom recognizes this and that is why she called Posey and not the rest of us for help. It doesn't mean she doesn't love us. It doesn't mean that she doesn't complain about Posey or not yell at her. I am in awe at how much love and energy Posey puts into taking care of Mom…Can we agree that selling Mom's house is the best for her estate?…

I hope you will each consider talking with Mom. Not about your own issues or about financial issues; she is beyond being able to deal with that. But talk about her and letting her know how much you love her. It doesn't need to be a long conversation…If you can help her remember something pleasant or funny and make her laugh, all the better…I love to make her laugh; it is so healing.

I love you all,

Rhonda

Soon after Rhonda's note, the messages I sent to Robin's email address came back undeliverable. Her feelings were clear. With the accusations against Rocky and me of trying to steal money and family heirlooms, sides were drawn. Ranelle, Robin and Tim all partnered together. They also believed I was making premature decisions on Mom's behalf. Ultimately, Renita and Rhonda and Rocky had enduring faith in my ability to care for our Mom and never questioned my honesty or integrity. Over the next few years, their love and support gave me the strength and confidence I needed to continue with my care of Mom.

## Surprise Visit

"Ranelle and Tim are going to be visiting me," Mom said as I walked into her room.

I didn't know how to respond. My brother and sister had not contacted me. I had no knowledge of any of my siblings coming to New York for a visit, which was surprising since I dropped in on Mom most every day.

"I didn't know that, Mom. Are you sure?" The words sputtered from my mouth.

"Yes, Tim called and told me."

"Do you know when?"

"I think soon."

Baffled, I tried to comprehend this news. Instantly, my anxiety rose as I contemplated a deceptive move on my sibling's part. *If Tim and Ranelle only told Mom of their impending visit, were they deliberately going behind my back? Or, did they simply feel they did not need to consult with me about visiting Mom?* With trembling hands, I contacted Renita, Rhonda and Rocky as I stepped into the hallway out of Mom's sight. With this report, my sisters became very alarmed. If Ranelle and Tim didn't want me to know they were visiting, then they must be up to something we assumed. *What if that something was a scheme to take Mom back to Indiana? We knew they believed* Ranelle could take care of Mom. Part of me felt *let them take her, let Ranelle have the responsibility.* But, my heart knew taking Mom from the home she had lived in for almost a year, one she had become comfortable and secure in, would cause her irreparable distress.

In the following days, a feeling of a gathering darkness loomed over us. With urgency, my sisters convinced me to file for full legal guardianship. This would give me the right to make all decisions regarding Mom's care.

Legally, however, Mom had the right and was given the opportunity to look over the Guardianship documents. Her lawyer's assistant delivered a huge manila envelope to Mom at Hawthorne Ridge while I was there. I stepped out of the room while the contents were explained to Mom. It was difficult for Mom to comprehend, because of her diminished mental capacity. Eventually, after the legal assistant left I wandered back into her room. I knew this would be very emotional for Mom; after all, who wants to relinquish control of their life? I thought I could explain the reasons and persuade Mom this was in her best interest. For an hour, I read and explained the legal documents to her in simpler terms than the legal assistant did. My intention was for Mom to realize her life was not going to change in any way. We would continue with her manicure appointments, lunch dates at our favorite diner, and my habitual delivery of chocolate with each visit.

"Mom would you like to meet with your lawyer?"

"No, I am fine with it Posey as long as you say nothing will truly change in how you take care of me."

"Mom, I promise I will continue to discuss your health and finances with you and ask you what you would like to do. This is protection for you so that no one else can step in and take over your care."

I thought that Mom was satisfied with the matter.

According to the law, the Guardianship documents had to be sent to all of my siblings. We assumed, but were not sure, that the packages would arrive the day before Ranelle and Tim left their homes for their unannounced visit. I felt better knowing that since the paperwork had been drawn up, although not yet finalized, Mom could not be legally taken out of the state.

A few days later when Ranelle and Tim arrived at Mom's place they called me and asked if I would come down so we could talk. I never expected them to contact me. My gut reaction was a fear of being manipulated and being pulled into a nasty argument. Paul's concern compelled him to accompany me.

Mom stayed in her room as the four of us sat in the alcove outside of her room. Ranelle and Tim looked me right in the eye and said that they supported me one hundred percent in the seeking of the Guardianship. As the conversation continued, they gave me the impression that they were okay with where Mom was now living. In my naivety, I felt relieved. In the end, Ranelle and Tim invited us to accompany them as they took Mom to dinner. Paul and I agreed but not without some trepidation.

We did not see Ranelle and Tim again during their weeklong visit. After they returned home, one afternoon, I decided to organize Mom's room. I came across the packet of documents from Mom's lawyer and looked inside and to my surprise, I found the business card of another local lawyer.

"Mom, what is this?"

"I don't know."

"Did Ranelle and Tim take you to see anyone while they were here?"

Mom looked confused; she hesitated like a small child who doesn't want to admit a wrong. I changed the subject.

"Did you have fun while Ranelle and Tim were here?"

"Not really, we spent a lot of time driving around Troy looking for an office."

There was my answer.

Although Ranelle and Tim stated they supported me, they failed to mention they consulted a lawyer. I assumed they did so to find out what their legal options were. I'll truly never know. What I was certain of, though, was that my initial gut reaction was correct and that I would be hard pressed to ever trust them again.

As our conversation continued, Mom queried me about the packet I held on my lap. She was asking new questions and focusing in on one word: incompetent. Before we had been in complete agreement; now that one word was about to come between us.

I drew in my breath and mustered my patience.

"Mom, it is just one word and I know that word contains a lot of meaning to you, but not to the lawyer who drew up the papers."

"But I am not incompetent. Why, if I wanted to, I could go get in my car and leave here." I had a feeling she knew this wasn't true, but I didn't push the point.

"Mom, let me ask you this. Do you like how I take care of you?"

"Yes."

"Do you like living here?" She looked around as she affirmed this, with a nod.

"Mom, I will still consult you on all decisions, I will still take you to all of your appointments. I will still visit you. Our relationship will not change."

"Okay, Posey, I trust you."

With Mom comfortably situated in her recliner I turned and walked out the door feeling emotionally exhausted yet satisfied she knew I only had her best interests in mind.

# Court

It had been a few days since Mom and I had reviewed and settled on the fact that my guardianship was going to be okay. But on my next visit, surprisingly, Mom had more questions. Her questions seemed strange to me, not ones she would have thought of on her own. This prompted me to check the call log of her phone. I discovered she was receiving daily calls from Ranelle, Tim and Robin. It seemed to me they were planting the seeds of doubt in Mom and persuading her to fight the guardianship. On each subsequent visit over the next two weeks, I would answer all her questions, calm Mom's fears, and settle any doubt she had. However, one day, Mom said she wanted to see her lawyer.

Ironically, while some of my siblings were coercing Mom to challenge the guardianship, she still relied on me for help. When Mom could not figure out how to use her phone to call her lawyer, I was the one who made the call and set up an appointment. This meeting led to what I assumed Ranelle, Robin and Tim wanted, Mom suing me over the Guardianship. Mom, however, only focused on the use of the word *incompetent,* written in just one paragraph out of probably a hundred pages. In her mind, the time in front of the judge would be about her concern over this word. During the course of the next few weeks, I was forced to hire my own lawyer, meet with him and, also take Mom to consult with her lawyer. I was pulled in many different directions, causing me a lot of time and distress. It was ludicrous.

On the day of Mom's appointment with her attorney, I drove a half hour from my home in Clifton Park to Hawthorne Ridge in East Greenbush to pick her up. I spent close to an hour getting her dressed and ready, and then helped her to my car. We drove forty-five minutes to the lawyer's office in Niskayuna, over two county lines. I helped Mom into the office and then retreated to a nearby Starbucks for one hour where I waited while Mom talked with her lawyer. After the appointment, we drove back to Hawthorne Ridge with a stop at Wendy's for a hamburger, another hour. I walked Mom back to her room and helped her get settled. Finally, I drove back home feeling the entire day was an out-of-body experience. I questioned myself: *When did I become the parent to my mother? How had my life become a battle with my mom and some of my siblings? But the most nagging question of all: Was there any logic to Mom's meeting with her lawyer?*

For weeks I agonized over the impending outcome of the court proceeding. I would fall asleep upon hitting my pillow only to be awakened hours later with thoughts of dreadful outcomes. I worried that if the guardianship failed, Mom would be convinced to move back to her house in Indiana. This decision would perhaps benefit some of my siblings but certainly not Mom.

Mom did not respond well to the stress either. She started to refuse to get out of bed in the mornings. She became mean with her comments to the staff and those around her. She lost her energy and walked more slowly. She stayed in her room with the curtains drawn and repeatedly read the same book.

Finally, the day arrived for Mom and me to sit before a judge and for her to explain her concerns. I was nervous because when I arrived to pick Mom up she was not dressed. Mom said she was too tired to complete the task on her own. This glitch made us a few minutes late.

The judge's small chambers was filled with attorneys and other legal personnel: my lawyer, Mom's lawyer, the lawyer appointed as her guardian by the courts, the judge and the court recorder. We sat down; the judge looked at both of us solemnly.

He asked Mom, "What objections if any, do you have to filing the guardianship?"

Although it was my belief three of my siblings had talked Mom into fighting with me in court, not one showed up on that day. Consequently, Mom stood alone in her confusion. Although asked about the guardianship she replied, "I do not like the wording that says I am incompetent."

The judge said, "I don't think it says that anywhere here in these papers."

That was when Mom's lawyer stepped in and explained that all her client was looking for was to not be declared incompetent. The judge agreed to Mom's request. He asked once again if she would consent to the guardianship.

With an affirmative nod from Mom, the proceeding ended with the guardianship being granted. Amazingly, the ordeal was over in just five minutes. Mom, herself a former judge, was happy about being able to tell this judge what she wanted. Her dignity was intact. In the end, we all agreed I would still consult Mom on decisions, as long as this was possible and that I could go ahead and sell Mom's house as recommended by her financial advisor. Sadly, Mom spent thousands of dollars for a fight she didn't really understand.

I drove home after making sure Mom was settled back at Hawthorne Ridge. I called my supportive siblings and delivered the good news, but I was finding it difficult to feel celebratory. I actually just wanted sit down and let the past few days drain from my body.

Two weeks later Paul and I took Mom out for dinner. I read in the newspaper that the judge we had appeared before was running for office. I said, "Mom, remember that judge we saw in court?"

She looked at me with a quizzical face. I rephrased the question. "Remember the judge we saw about the guardianship?"

She looked at me strangely and replied. "No, I don't remember."

I felt the wave of that statement rush against my body. I looked around. *Had anyone else just felt that jolt in the Earth's axis? Was I the only one who felt time had stopped for just a nanosecond?* Mom did not remember our own personal courtroom drama! The realities of those stress-filled days were gone for her. It occurred to me she did not seem to have any worries and, in fact, was just enjoying an enormously big hamburger, the moment, and the company of her daughter and son-in-law.

## Selling Mom's House

I received a check in the mail from the appraiser who sold the contents of my mother's house. I did not go to the auction. Mom had not lived in her home for almost two years. As Mom's guardian, I, along with the input of some of my siblings decided to sell Mom's house.

My sister Renita, a realtor, put the house on the market. She flew to Indiana from Oregon and walked through our childhood home with a realtor's eye. She hired painters, repair people and a cleaning staff. Because she could not stay, Renita hired a local realtor to sell the house. The whole process took several months. Throughout, Renita kept me updated with phone calls and emails.

Our family pictures and keepsakes were boxed up by me Rocky and Renita during different visits to work on the house and mailed to all seven siblings. We tried to consider everyone's feelings and went out of our way to save even the slightest memento. We placed other items in storage to be divided among us after Mom's passing.

In the months before the sale, many of us had arranged to take items we wanted most. I took the table my family sat at for dinner. When I was a freshman in high school, my best friend moved away. I spent that summer missing her terribly so I refinished the family table and the buffet that went with it.

During holiday meals, we crowded around the table that was oozing food. At Thanksgiving, it was a massive turkey with oyster stuffing and frozen cranberry salad. At Christmas, there were always more cookies than the table could hold. On Easter, we loved the ham complemented by pickled eggs and beets. During the summer, I remember racing to a seat after being outside all day, to down a full glass of milk and gobble up fresh corn and tomatoes.

My sisters had connections to other family heirlooms. Rhonda took our grandfather's secretary desk and the antique books inside. She loves to read, she and Mom had that bond.  She also took the spinning wheel that family lore says came over from Ireland. Rocky took the oak bookcase with the glass front, which became Mom's when she retired from teaching. Mom had used the bookcase every day she taught at the high school and had always admired it. One day it showed up on our front porch, a gift from the janitor. I am not sure the principal ever knew what happened.

The grandchildren took the games, worn with decades of use. Long afternoons had been spent playing with Grandmom. She was a fierce competitor. They were not allowed to win just because they were young. "Better to learn early that nothing in life is given to you," Mom always said to them.

A few days before the closing, Paul and I made one final trip. We donated the remaining clothing and household items to the local theater and charities. We had a dumpster delivered and anything leftover was thrown out. The whole process was exhausting, both physically and mentally.

In the end, I believed I was fine with all of this. After all, it is just a house. No one in the family wanted it. Except for my brother, not one of us still lived in Indiana. The appraiser packed up Mom's remaining possessions. He loaded her belongings into trucks, took them away and sold them at an auction. Not one person from my family was present.

I had felt that everything of value, monetary or emotional had been taken out of the house. That day the check came, I thought, *Oh, I forgot this was coming.*

I took the envelope to my office and opened it. Out fell the check and a list of everything that had been sold. Suddenly, my throat constricted and my eyes welled with tears. I was so sure I was okay with this arrangement, yet there I sat reading and crying over old furniture no one wanted. The desk chair my father had bought in New York, loaded into his van, and transported across half of the country to get it back to Indiana. The bed my parents had slept in. The couches where Mom and I had sat, laughing together, while watching the *Late Show with David Letterman.*

Some paperweight that had sold for a very good price, I didn't even recall. *Should I have kept it?* A wave of guilt rushed over me. Since I was the Guardian, I had made the decision to sell all of this. Perhaps I should have been more conscientious. After all, what is valuable and what is not? When you can no longer grab hold of something, does that suddenly make it more precious? Emotionally, I was shattered to know that I had a hand in dismantling my family home: That the house my family lived in was no longer as we remembered it. The house still stands, but not the contents, nor the laughter, nor the love, not even the bad times. My childhood home was gone.

All that was left was the check I held in my hand.

Family home
the day it was sold
2009

The fireplace where so
many family pictures were taken

## Selling Mom's Car

The 1995 Lincoln Town Car that I drove Mom to New York in was still sitting in our driveway. The vehicle had lived a good life of over ten years with my parents' gentle care. It was red with a red leather interior. Even though it was old, it had many of the gadgets that today's newer cars have like intermittent wipers, automatic locks, windows and headlights. The car was huge; the front end was approximately the size of a Mini Cooper, which may explain its pick-up. The car floated over the road handling bumps as if they weren't even there.

Parking was difficult. Many of today's lots are tighter. The Lincoln needed a huge amount of area to first swing out and then maneuver the front end into a parking space. I often had to back up and readjust. I got strange looks as I drove, especially when I was alone. I know most people presumed an elderly person was at the wheel of the car. It was obvious they imagined I would be moving slowly so many cars pulled out in front of me. Or, at four way stops, they would wave instructions to me when it was my turn, believing I was a senile senior who needed help. I grew accustomed to this, and even though at first I hated chauffeuring Mom around in her Lincoln, it became something I just did to make her feel more at home.

During the last two years Mom owned the Lincoln, between storage, insurance and upkeep, she spent more than the car was worth. It had close to 150,000 miles on it and needed new brakes. It was time to sell. I had mixed emotions about this. Every time I picked Mom up in her car she exclaimed, "Isn't this a beautiful car? Don't you just love driving it? It sure does ride nice."

I discussed with her the reasons why she needed to sell her car. She agreed with me, but because of her dementia, she consistently forgot our conversations. I was left with the guilt of making the decision to sell her beloved car.

Eventually I listed Mom's car online. I had a few people call, but no one offered anything reasonable. Finally, a guy called and came for a test drive. He knew a lot about Lincolns and seemed very interested. I wasn't sure I liked him. It was apparent he was a used car dealer trying to get a cheap deal from me. I consulted my Angels and asked for help in dealing with this man. When he offered half of what we asked, and then rudely called back several times to tell us we were wrong in not selling him the car, I knew I was given my answer. The next day we got another call. I could tell from caller ID that it was coming from a body shop in nearby Troy. I thought, *this is just another angle that used car salesman is trying,* but it was not. Instead, a young couple came over and to look at the car. They were genuinely excited.

> This is just what we are looking for. We are surprised that the car is in the shape you claimed it would be in your ad. So many people are not honest about their cars. When you go to look at them it is not even worth the drive you made.

They were expecting their first baby and they wanted a safe car for the wife to drive. The husband was knowledgeable about Lincolns because his family owned the body shop. They knew they could repair the minor dents and dings.

As they were looking the car over, I reflected, *Okay, I would feel good about selling Mom's car to this couple, people who were eager to own it and treat it well.*

I know that sounds ridiculous, it was just a car. But, my memories of Mom and Dad enjoying themselves as they drove all over the country were ingrained in my mind. Mom had such affection for it. There had been many changes and losses in her life; selling this automobile was one more. I was going back and forth in my mind with my feelings of guilt when the phone rang. It was my sister, Rocky.

"What are you doing?"

"Actually, I think I just sold Mom's car, but I feel guilty."

"Oh, honey you shouldn't feel that. You and Mom have discussed this."

"But she loves that car; she always talks about how nice it is."

Are you sure she doesn't just say that because Dad always did? Maybe it's just something she says whenever she rides in it because she doesn't really know what else to say. She probably will not remember the car if it is gone. Just tell her that you sold the Lincoln as you had discussed. She will understand.

Tears filled my eyes, but I felt relief. I knew my sister was right. I also knew this was the sign from my Angels telling me to go through with the sale.

When the couple came and picked up Mom's car, I cried as I watched it back down the driveway one last time. I strained to watch it go around the corner and out of sight. I consoled myself with the thought of how happy the new owners seemed. I made a wish that they would enjoy the car as much as Mom and Dad had.

The Lincoln parked outside my home
Clifton Park, NY

## Worry

My life with Mom continued its slow slide into nothing. Some days Mom's care consumed me and at times, I was pulled into depths of despair. I was anxious about things not in my control. I was troubled about following my mother's footsteps into dementia. Strangely, I was not worried about myself, or how that might feel. I was not concerned with the struggle I would feel as my mind slipped away. Instead, I fretted about my children having to take care of me.

It was ironic I was bothered about that, because I did not resent taking care of my mother. I related it to changing a baby's diaper. The task itself is not pleasant. In fact, at times it is gross. When you love the baby whose diaper you are changing all of the unpleasantness is irrelevant. The same was true of my mother. One day she was at my house. Just as I was getting ready to put dinner on the grill, Mom needed to go to the bathroom. I helped her in. I waited outside the door because I knew she frequently did not wash her hands and I would need to remind her as one would a child. As she came out the door I asked, "Mom did you wash your hands?" She rolled her eyes just like a teenager.

"Why are you always so concerned about whether I wash my hands?"

"For one thing we are going to eat dinner soon; the other is hand washing helps to keep you from getting sick."

She went back in and ran water over her hands; I'm sure she did not use soap. Later I went in to the bathroom and noticed there was urine all over the toilet seat. I cleaned it up, and throughout this whole process, I wondered to myself, *why doesn't this bother me? I know it will bother me if my children have to clean up after me. Why did I feel this was different?*

I loved my mother, but we were never close enough for me to feel I could be totally open with her. I knew I could never tell her some parts of my life, without a huge lecture. Once while she still lived with me, I related a funny story about a party I attended in college. She barked, "If I had known you were drinking in college I never would have paid your tuition."

I thought, *still in trouble at fifty years old.*

Since Mom and I never bonded with girl talk, I always hoped I would have a better relationship with my own daughters. I worked hard over the years to achieve that fine balance of mother, but not too over bearing. As my daughters matured, our relationship grew along with us. We laughed about stupid jokes. They conveyed stories about their friends. They asked me if their outfits looked right, and I did the same. At times, I found myself thinking *how unbearable it would be to not be able to enjoy their company anymore.*

I worried that if I started down the same path of dementia, I would lose that friendship with my girls. I was concerned I would miss the phone calls when there was a crisis. I wanted to be the one they came to with exciting news. If I followed in my Mom's footsteps I wouldn't be able to hear the gossip of their lives. I did not want the day to come when my daughters would need to look after me. This was and still is my gravest fear.

**Questions about Dad**

On many occasions when I visited Mom, I found her in her room watching MSNBC. I was not sure how much she could follow, but throughout her life, she always liked to be up on current events. One afternoon we were watching together when out of nowhere she asked, "I wonder where Joe is?"

"What do you mean?"

Questions wandered through my head: *Did she mean my Dad? Where is he buried? Was she wondering if he was still alive?*

"Well I just wonder what happened to him."

"Mom, Dad passed away eight years ago."

"That would explain a lot," she said, matter of factly.

"If he were still alive he would be checking up on me."

"He would be here living with you, Mom." I said with some melancholy.

I could tell by the way she looked at me, with an expression of doubt, that she wasn't quite sure I was telling her the truth. As gently as I could, I explained Dad's passing.

"Mom, Dad had a heart attack and then open heart surgery, but he never truly recovered from it. Even before he had the surgery there was something wrong with his lungs, the doctors couldn't figure it out, and so his lungs just stopped working."

She nodded, but did not say a word.

"He died in February of 2001."

"Was I there?"

"Yes, you were there with Rocky and Ranelle."

"Before he died, Rocky promised that she and I would take care of you, Mom. That is why you are here with me now."

"So he knew he was dying?"

"Yes, I think so"

Sadly, Mom did not recall the last days of Dad's life. That Rocky, arriving from her home in Georgia found both Mom and Ranelle paralyzed with exhaustion and indecision. Assessing the situation, Rocky realized she would need to be the one to guide them towards the decision to remove Dad from life support. Before he was taken off the machines he never would have wanted, Rocky whispered in his ear, "Dad, you can let go, I promise to take care of Mom."

I should have been there to help Rocky, but a certain part of me is glad I was not. My last image of my father was the smile he gave me as I walked out of his hospital room just three weeks earlier, a picture I treasure.

There was silence in the room. I could tell Mom wanted more information.

"Mom, Dad is buried in Wabash where you both lived. He lived there his whole life."

She was struggling so I described his tombstone.

"Mom, the front has two sides; on one side are Dad's name and a list of some of his accomplishments, like World War II veteran, Judge, Irishman. On the other side is your name with a list of your accomplishments, like educator and counselor. The back of the stone lists the names of all of your children."

"It sounds very nice and thoughtful. Who took care of all of that?"

"You did, Mom."

I could tell this last statement made her proud, but with sadness and a question on her face she said, "I just don't remember."

Mom and Dad
1974

Leisure suit era
1970s

1987

An evening out
October 1993

Christmas morning
1960s

Mom and Dad formal portrait
1990s

Lunch at home
1970s

Mom with video camera
early 1990s

Formal Portrait
1990s

At a Judge's Convention
1990s

1990

1990s

Mom's birthday
her favorite chocolate cake
1990s

Special night out
1990s

## From Our View

If I didn't find Mom sitting in her recliner feet propped up watching the news then I would wander through her community home and find her involved in an activity. It might be a barbeque or listening to a choral group, perhaps decorating for a holiday. Sometimes it was dancing or maybe sharing a quiet evening of old movies with new friends. For the most part, the residents of Hawthorne Ridge seemed to participate at varying levels in most activities. Some enjoyed the events with gusto; others sat and observed, often with smiles on their face. The personnel knew each resident by name and often encouraged involvement.

Hawthorne Ridge was a great community. The staff was caring and knowledgeable. As mental health professionals dealing with dementia patients, they constantly tried to provide new opportunities for those trusted to their care. Wanting to keep family members up to date, the director held quarterly meetings. It took me a year and a half to subdue the sadness I often felt when visiting Mom and work up the courage to attend one of these meeting. At first, I rationalized my absences by using my substitute teaching schedule as an excuse. Or, I justified my nonattendance with the need to spend as many evenings as possible with my daughter, Kristen during her last year living at home. But after several months, I realized I had run out of excuses, and my fears needed to be put to the wayside. I put the quarterly meeting on my calendar.

When the day arrived, I showed up in time to have a sandwich with some of the other family members I had seen around the home. We casually chatted. Eventually, our conversation turned to our loved ones and the inevitable questions that were always asked.

How is your mother doing?

Do you think your dad has declined at all?

Has your husband had any major illnesses?

These were just some of the questions we all faced. I was concerned about a parent, others a beloved spouse. We all saw them falling into the nothingness of dementia and we couldn't pull them out; we could only watch their descent. Sometimes we watched with horror, other times it was with humor because without humor, we had learned that the days became nothing but dread and sorrow.

The meeting began and the director was bubbling with information about a new program called The Box Concept. It sounded wonderful. The idea was to fill boxes with objects designed to keep idle hands busy and to stimulate memories. There would be tools to work with, laundry to fold and any number of items to sort from scraps of material to new socks. One box may contain wooden blocks to paint with the finished product being donated to local children's hospitals. Dolls would be available for women who needed to feel their arms full once again. There were cooking utensils, crafts - the list was endless. The staff learned to identify when residents were feeling uneasy or restless and grow to recognize which box they enjoyed most and provide it to them.

As a mature adult, I fully understood the concept. It reminded me of some of the techniques I used while teaching in elementary schools. But as the child of a mother who lived in this specialized community, I also felt sadness.

The staff played a short video showing how the project would work and it ended with scenes of dementia patients enjoying the different stations. The song that accompanied the video was heartrending, *Remember Me, Do Not Forget Who I Was*. Some of us began to cry. Our tears were for the future that was stolen from us by this cruel disease. We were saddened to think of conversations that would never happen; adult children contemplated missing a reassuring hug from a parent; spouses longed for a loving, passionate kiss, or the simple act of holding hands.

The staff seemed confused by our tears. They were all excited anticipating the families would welcome this new program. This is where the road divided. The staff saw our family members as they were, as patients they were trying very hard to help. We saw them as they once were and knew exactly what they could no longer be or do. Every day we faced the knowledge that we were slowly losing a loved one. We agreed this new program would bring joy, comfort, perhaps that feeling once again of accomplishing a simple task. Still, our tears were for us, for the stories we'd never hear again, and the longing for melodic laughter over remembered jokes.

**Out of Control**

By spring of 2009, I was out of control. Papers were piling up. I couldn't find the top of my desk. As I sat in a daze of confusion and frustration, my eyes wandered to the organized chaos of stacked documents and files sitting all over my home office. The mess spilled onto the floor and the tabletop, even the couch. One day as I sat in the middle of this chaos, I heard the un-wanted sound of the mail truck causing my apprehension to rise.

Getting organized was a priority but I truly felt I needed more time for my writing, which always served as a way to release my anxieties.

I had a myriad of tasks to complete that I frequently procrastinated on because I hated doing them. I needed to pay our bills and also Mom's. Little things took so much time: Why had the cable company automatically deducted money from Mom's checking account when I paid the bills by check? Why had her newspaper suddenly stopped being delivered? More importantly, my list included finding all of the paperwork for Mom's taxes and filling out the forms for her accountant. I even needed to plan ahead and set money aside for Mom's funeral. According to Mom's instructions, each child, grandchild, and great-grandchild was to be allocated money from her estate to cover all travel expenses to her funeral.

Accomplishing these tasks, both big and small, weighed heavily on me. Self-imposed guilt trips to visit Mom harassed me daily.

I wanted to be there for my daughters and support them as they made real life decisions about jobs and internships. Emotionally, I was spent.

Of course, there was always the day to day: laundry, the grocery, and never time to work out. I longed for the chance to relax and more joy in my life. It was at this time, that a family ski vacation in Colorado presented itself.

My dilemma was which siblings could travel to my home to be available for Mom in my absence? Although logistically complicated, I could bring in family members for short periods of time, coordinating schedules with others to fill the week time span. No one stepped up for a variety of what I considered lame reasons except Rocky, who offered. I refused because I did not want her to miss yet another one of her children's school events.

It depressed me that I had to beg for help when I felt my siblings should realize how taxing full responsibility of Mom was. I wished they could get together and figure out who was going to do what and when, and surprise me with a plan. In the end, our niece, Leanne, rearranged her schedule, leaving behind her husband and two young children to come to our rescue.

That week in Summit County, Colorado was worth it. I was finally prioritizing in a positive and healthy way. Despite my sibling's lack of assistance, and knowing the paperwork would always be there waiting, I learned that if I took care of me, I could take better care of Mom.

## In Search of the Perfect Burger

My mother loved hamburgers. She loved them thick and juicy, with ripe tomato slices, lots of salt and, most importantly, a thick slice of raw red onion. Finding a hamburger made to her specifications was not a simple task. Certainly, you did not get this at McDonald's. Over the course of a year, I took my mother to several restaurants in search of her perfect burger. Mom perused each menu carefully.

"All of these burgers have too much stuff on them, I want mine just basic."

"Mom, they will make yours anyway you like, order what you want."

I optimistically assumed this local, well patronized diner, would be the place where Mom found a hamburger that fit her craving. When her sandwich arrived, off came the bun for inspection.

"Well, this isn't a slice of onion, this is just pieces."

"Don't you think that pieces of onion will taste the same as a whole slice?"

She gave me a look as if to say, *are you an idiot*? The whole meal was ruined; on only complaints followed. Sometimes the waitress might bring lettuce when she didn't order it, or the tomatoes were not ripe, perhaps missing altogether. But the biggest complaint was always about the onion.

Let down again, I ate my meal hoping in the future to find a restaurant that would fulfill my mother's desire.

Confidently, on another outing I took my mother to a different diner, one near her Hawthorne Ridge home, where they claimed to have the best burgers around. They even described the type of toppings my Mom liked. She ordered, and I waited in anticipation. When her plate arrived she followed her routine and removed the bun. No complaints, the onion looked all in order. She picked up the hamburger dripping in grease, oozing tomatoes and topped nicely with fresh iceberg lettuce.

"The bun is cold," she exclaimed. I said nothing. "I can't get my mouth around the whole burger, it is too big."

She dropped the entire thing on her plate with disgust. It was then, after many visits to hamburger joints around the Capital District it hit me: *Mom would never be satisfied with any hamburger.*

Mom, at least in later years of her life, was a complainer. I knew this but chose to deny it. She was never happy. Nothing was ever right. I wondered: *was she like this all of her life? Her nickname was Corki, how would someone who did not enjoy life get that name? When did she became like this?*

I recalled the humorous story my Mom told of when she was young, about how her grandmother had fallen and couldn't get herself back on her feet. I thought about when she and her girlfriend Tommy traveled across the country, it was the adventure of a life time. Mom was a teacher and I remembered how her face revealed true happiness when recollecting how the staff sat around and divulged amusing tales of their student's exploits. Throughout her life so many people enjoyed her company.

So I wondered. At what point in time did Mom lose the ability to laugh? I imagined it was having seven children and bills that needed to be paid along with working full time and dealing with my father's excessive drinking. It made me sad. I concluded I needed to reconcile myself to the fact Mom had not been happy for years and I couldn't change that. She could no longer understand how to find joy. She wallowed in her gloom. I came to this realization perhaps late. I had disappointed myself more than once expecting to see a smile appear on Mom's face and needed to hear *thanks, this is the best burger I've had in a long time*. With that knowledge, I no longer sought to make her happy, thus disappointing myself once again.

Although there were many more visits to area restaurants, I was no longer in search of the perfect burger.

## My Neighbor Bill

One morning as I was out walking, I ran into my neighbor, Bill. I wanted to be just like him. Retirement agreed with him. Bill rode around his yard on his spring green John Deere lawn tractor that he used to fertilize and mow. In late winter, he started seedlings for all the flowers that would fill his yard come spring, making his yard as colorful as a box of Crayons. His annual gardens caused neighbors to stop and drivers to slow down and take pause.

As he worked in his yard, Bill often spent time chatting with passersby and that is how we met. In my Purdue sweatshirt, I hurried down the street with my exercise gait in full swing. He shouted to me, "Are you really a Purdue person?"

"Yes, my husband and I are both graduates."

"Well, so am I, though my wife went to that *other* school, Indiana University."

Thus began our friendship. Bill always had something to talk about. In the fall, it was the Purdue football team.

"Did you watch the game on Saturday? What do you think of the new coach? How about Drew Brees and the Saints, Purdue sure can turn out a good quarterback."

During the winter, we discussed basketball and that year there were many exciting Purdue games and players to discuss.

"I think Purdue just might make it to the final four." Bill almost whispered to avoid a jinx on the team.

Much later in the season after Purdue had beaten the local favorite, Siena College, we both bragged a little louder. Finally, though, when our star player injured himself, we commiserated.

"Sorry to hear about Robbie. I think we could have gone all the way if he hadn't torn that ACL."

I nodded and the two of us silently reflected about our lost hope and the heartbreak of following Purdue teams.

Bill knew about business and management. He worked for several years at General Electric. He kept himself abreast of the latest news and information. He had traveled all over the world.

"Australia was one of my favorite countries. I would move there in a heartbeat if not for my family. The last time I was there with my wife I told her I want to go downtown and watch all the pretty girls go by." He chuckled, remembering. Then his face took on a somber look as he recollected his last few years with GE.

"But then GE told me for three years straight to lay ten percent of my people off. Every year I said I would, but I didn't. Finally, after the third year I knew I couldn't continue telling the head honchos one thing and doing another so I retired."

I noticed a sly grin on his face as he looked around at his yard and garden.

"But that hasn't been so bad." Abruptly Bill mentioned, "Today's my birthday."

"Do you mind if I ask how old you are?"

"No, I don't mind if you ask," he said toying with me.

What followed was silence between us as the birds chirped and cars drove by. Finally, I noticed he had a smirk on his face and a twinkle in his eye. It occurred to me he was waiting for me to ask.

"How old are you, Bill?"

"I am eighty-two today."

"Congratulations."

Later, as I walked up the hill to my house, I thought *I want to be like Bill when I get to be eighty-two*. Bill and I talked many times and I never noticed the thirty years difference in our ages. He was aware of the world around him and his place in it. He has not succumbed to thinking like an old person. I never heard Bill talk about the younger generation in a negative way. He always had something positive to say. I was sure, like all of us as we age, he had aches and pains but you would never know it as he worked in his yard.

Yet there was something more in my observations, something tucked away in my soul. Daily at Hawthorne Ridge I was surrounded by people Bill's age with dementia - once brilliant people like him, who had literally lost their minds.

I knew, as with all living creatures the brain controls the body. With dementia, the mind slowly betrays you as you revert back to a child. As you mentally slip away, there are times you know what will eventually happen. You understand you will no longer be able to walk or talk. You know bodily functions will not be controlled; eventually swallowing will become too difficult. You realize what a burden you will be to your family, how difficult it will be for them. Yet, you are powerless to change it. This was my fear; I didn't want to leave this life with dementia. So I prayed. Let me be just like my neighbor, Bill.

## Comfort

One day on my way back into Mom's room after refilling her bird feeder, I ran into a woman I had become friends with, Margy. Her mom, Peggy, and my Mom were friends. Neither talked much, but they had established a bond. I could tell Peggy, at one time, shared the same kind of spunk and sense of humor my Mom once did.

Margy visited her Mom daily and helped her eat her lunch. I knew Margy struggled with other very critical issues in her life, yet she always had a smile for me. She'd asked how I was doing. We both knew the inner battles we were going through: how it hurt to visit and how the guilt was ever present when we not able to get there. Sometimes ignoring everyone else was easier than confronting the awful demon of dementia. Through Margy's example, I began to reach out to the other families. These people were part of my life and Mom's; I could no longer disregard them.

Each family member coped in a different way. One woman I met managed by showing up every day for one of the meals. She knew the staff and felt they could use her help. She had taken the time to get to know each resident by name. She bustled about getting coffee and turning on the jukebox for some dinner music. I think it must have pained her to see her mother struggle to eat, but she compensated by helping all of the residents and taking charge of organizing the drinks and music.

Other families withdrew into themselves and sat quietly with their loved ones. Perhaps, like I once was, it was too much to take on the burden of others. Coping with their own sorrows was more than enough.

Once I began to connect with others, I realized we had a common bond of families living with dementia. With a knowing glance, we acknowledged the stress of being in this painful and unwanted chapter. We knew a lot about each other even if we just exchanged hellos.

## Another Mother

One afternoon I received a call from the staff of Hawthorne Ridge. They informed me that Mom was ill, nothing serious, just a virus going through the residence. The next day I bought Mom some flowers and went to visit. When I walked in her room, she was sleeping. I had opened the door slowly so I would not wake her, but she opened her eyes and smiled at me. I returned the smile.

"Hey Mom, I came down to check on you, to see how you are doing."

She blinked her eyes and stretched out lazily. She raised her arms above her head and extended her legs; she stirred in a seductive way. It all seemed unusual. Because of her arthritis, Mom normally moved very slowly and painfully. But, as I watched, she stirred in the bed with the liquid fluidity of a young woman. Mom produced a peculiar smile and with self-importance she slowly asked, "Did you see my new baby boy?"

I was confused. *Was she referring to the new stuffed animal she had won at Bingo a few days ago?* "What baby, Mom?"

"I had a new baby boy last night," she said with boastful pride.

I was reluctant to hear her reply when I hesitantly asked, "What is his name?"

"Tim," she replied.

I staggered. My brother, Tim, was now in his forties. Shocked, I realized I was looking at my eighty-four year old mother, but in her mind she was a younger woman of forty-two; a woman who had just delivered the long-awaited boy after six consecutive girls. Tim would be the final child born to Corki and Joe Christle. I watched as she repositioned herself again, with contentment and self-pride. She had a smirk on her face of a job well done. I could almost hear her thinking *now I have accomplished my goal. I am truly fulfilled.*

Most children think of their parents as old. My big sisters spoke of a mom who did cartwheels on the front lawn. I never knew that person. As the true middle child, Mom was knee-deep in family care as I remember. Our fun times together were more practical consisting of me standing on a kitchen chair stirring the tomato soup as she made the grilled cheese sandwiches for lunch.

Yet, here at this moment, instead of an octogenarian, was a woman full of life. Mom oozed self-importance, aware that she had finally given her husband the boy they had so desired, the pinnacle of their family. As she moved in the bed, stretching and talking to me about her baby, resentment crept into my conscience. I begrudged the fact Mom had chosen the delivery of Tim to remember for many legitimate reasons. *Oh, if Tim had only lived up to their vision for him.* Jealousy boiled within me. *Why not relive the birth of one of us girls?* So much was always expected of us but Tim played by another set of rules.

I regained my composure. I tried to watch and perhaps catch a glimpse of the mother I never knew. By witnessing Mom relive that milestone; I felt I might understand her more as a whole woman. This day she was reliving was a highlight in her life. I could see it in her expressions. I did not recall ever seeing that look of contentment on my mother's face. She was serene.

Then I felt a jolt hit my heart. *Mom was happy*! I had been given the gift of seeing Mom joyful, something I had longed for, but truly thought I would never see. It was eerie to be in this situation. It was difficult to look at my elderly mother lying in front of me and try to relate to the younger woman she believed she was at that moment.

Blissfully she whispered, "Was he sleeping when you saw him?"

"Yes, Mom, he was," I stuttered.

Even though I continued to call her Mom, I could tell she did not see me as her grown daughter. I am not sure who she thought I was, probably just a visitor bringing her congratulatory flowers. She rolled over then, very easily; no groaning, no disjointed movements, a simple roll to her side that could easily be accomplished by the younger woman she had become.

Astonished, I backed out of the room and stood in the hallway a few moments to take in the event. I had to let my brain absorb the emotions my soul felt. I received a gift: a hint of the woman about whom I had been told stories. The woman who defied her father and married the man she was in love with, a poor Catholic boy. This was the young girl my father said lit up a room when she entered, the one he fell in love with the first time they danced. Here was the college girl who, along with her girlfriend, traveled across the United States during World War II. I finally caught a peek of the woman who lived up to the nickname "Corki."

Mom went back to sleep painfully resuming the physical traits of a person her age. As I walked away I couldn't help but think *I would have enjoyed the company of this remarkable woman.*

Mom in hospital when
she had Tim
1965

Mom and Tim
leaving hospital
1965

## Hospital Nightmare

Mom had been living at Hawthorne Ridge almost two years and we had become complacent with the arrangement. One weekend in September of 2009, I joined Paul in a quick visit to his sister's house in Rochester, New York. As we were enjoying an enormous Sunday breakfast in the local diner my cell phone rang. It was the nurse from Hawthorne Ridge.

"Your mom was leaning over today from her bed to pick something up off the floor. She dislocated her hip. We are sending her to the Emergency Room."

"Oh my God, is she in pain?"

"Yes, she has some pain. Her physical therapist found her. Can you meet her in the Emergency Room?"

"I, I'm in Rochester," I stammered. "It will take me at least three and a half hours to get back."

"Is there anyone else?"

"No, well yes, I will find someone."

The eggs in my stomach like those on my plate began to congeal making me feel instantly ill. In my mind, I desperately searched for a replacement until I could arrive. I settled on the one choice that made sense, my friend Jane, a nurse and mother of four, who has lot of common sense. She is always cool in a crisis.

Jane answered her cell phone as she was leaving church and, as I expected, abandoned her plans and family and headed right over to the hospital. Paul and I said our hurried good-byes, jumped in our car where, fortunately we already had our packed bags and sped our way to the Thruway and a nonstop drive from the central part of the state back east to Albany and Mom. Even with hair-raising speed that allowed us to arrive far before we anticipated, the drive still seemed endless to me. As we drove, I felt a growing panic rising in my throat. Not only was I feeling terrible about Mom's fall, but, truth be told in four days, Paul and I had tickets to board a plane. Our plan was to spend time with family and friends at our annual Purdue football weekend back in Indiana. I was desperate to go; as caretaker for Mom I needed a break and had been counting the days. I prayed: *Let this will all work out, so I can still go.*

When we arrived, Mom, who had been given painkillers,was dozing on a gurney and Jane sat beside her reading *People*. Jane updated us as we scurried in. It turned out that on this particular Sunday the Emergency Room was packed; there had been a severe multi-car accident. Mom was still waiting to be seen by a doctor. Jane left and Paul and I began a twelve-hour endurance test. I began to time when Mom was given painkillers so that before she became too uncomfortable I could start to search out a doctor to give her more. I hated to keep her drugged because too much medication causes dementia patients to lose brain function that never returns, but I had no choice.

Finally, an intern came in, looked at Mom and ordered X-rays. We waited for another hour until at last an aide came and took Mom for her X-rays. As I followed behind, I kept repeating to everyone I felt should know, "You realize this is her hip that was surgically replaced."

When we returned, a nurse approached. "Oh, there she is. The doctor was looking for her, but now he has moved on to another patient." I bit my tongue trying not to scream at the miscommunication among the staff. Paul and I sat in that tiny room, on sticky, hard plastic chairs for several more hours. At one point, Paul went home to get us more comfortable clothing and some food.

After waiting all day with no contact from the staff and therefore no information as to what was happening, a doctor came in. Instead of giving us his undivided attention as Paul and I tried to voice the fact Mom had dementia and that this was a surgically replaced hip, he simply grunted. It was obvious he wasn't listening to our concerns as he continued to look at a message on his cell phone. The doctor then stated that he was going to try to pop Mom's hip back into its socket.

"Since this requires some manipulation and this is a small room, you should step outside."

I took his advice. Looking through the tiny window of the closed door, I winced when they gave Mom a shot of even more pain medication, but she did not appear to feel a thing. I was glad I had stepped out of the room when the doctor began to work Mom's hip back into the socket. It almost seemed as if he would knock her off the gurney with his twisting and shoving. When the doctor finished I returned to the small room and he informed us that everything looked good.

"Did her left foot always turn at that angle?"

"Somewhat, but not to that extreme."

"Well, I am sure it is fine; we will do another X-ray and go from there."

The intern looked at me knowingly, but left with the doctor. An hour later after reading the new X-ray, the doctor was back in the room for another try at getting Mom's hip in place. The second time things worked out much better.

Exhausted and emotionally drained I thought we were out of the woods and I began to dream of a tall glass of wine and a hot bath. But none of that was in the cards for me for several days to come.

The intern was back. "So, we are going to release your Mom. Does she live with you?"

"No, she lives in an assisted living home."

"Well, the doctor wants her to wear this brace for twenty-four hours, just to make sure her hip doesn't pop back out. We have sent for the technician, it shouldn't be too long."

After another hour and a half wait, the technician, who had obviously been summoned from sleep, showed up. He brought with him an apparatus that looked like a medieval torture contraption. After wrestling Mom into the device I thought he was either going to knock her off her gurney or pop her hip back out. Thankfully, Mom was so drugged up she was like a rag doll and simply rolled and jerked in the directions he pushed her. I was horrified. Finally, he was satisfied with the results. There was no way for Mom to move her entire leg from her hip to the foot. The only position she could manage was lying down.

"How am I supposed to get her into a car?"

"Not sure. I am thinking we should admit her for the night and then when it is removed tomorrow, she can go home."

"Okay, but only for overnight. Otherwise, Mom has to be readmitted into her home by the doctor there and I don't want to deal with that."

"No problem." His spoken words were my kiss of death.

It was somewhere around one in the morning. I had been at the hospital at least since early afternoon, Mom even longer. I sent Paul home; no sense in both of us staying all night. I knew I had to be Mom's voice here in the hospital where she would be even more confused. I followed Mom through the winding maze that makes up the long-standing teaching hospital to her room. I lost track of which elevator I rode or exactly which floor we were on. The nurses were competent in their work, but they brushed aside my concerns about Mom and her dementia while sleeping in a new place. When it became apparent I had no intention of leaving, I could see the look of distrust on their faces. The only chair in Mom's room was, yet again, a hard plastic one. No one offered me anything else. After struggling not to fall out of the chair as I dozed, I finally gave in and found a waiting room. Here there were chairs with cushions so I pushed two together and managed a couple hours of rest.

The next morning, my nightmare continued. Apparently, there was a significant disagreement between the Emergency Room doctor and the hospital orthopedic of how long the brace should be worn. When I began to question Mom's release that day the nurses proclaimed they had heard nothing of it.

It was Monday; I needed to be on the plane by Thursday.

Mom woke and began to complain that the brace was hurting her back. Of course it did, it was wrapped around her waist with a large, thick belt, which did not allow her to lie flat. The nurses didn't want to raise the head of her bed, due to the brace, Mom couldn't sit up. A physical therapist was called in. She was supposed to get Mom out of bed and walk her around. She took one look at Mom and called for backup; now two of them could not figure out how to help Mom sit or stand. They couldn't even get her to the bathroom. Out of frustration, they removed the brace thinking they would put it back on her once she was standing. The problem was, they couldn't figure out how to do that. Mom was gently placed back in bed without the brace.

"We are going to have the technician return and show us how this brace works. Until then, don't let your Mom move around a lot."

I spent the rest of Monday hoping to talk with a doctor and waiting for the technician. Neither showed up, leaving Mom without the brace until the following day. Exhausted, I knew I could not spend another night sleeping on a cold plastic chair. Mom believed she was back at Hawthorne Ridge where she always stayed in bed all night until her aides woke her for breakfast. I took a chance that she would be okay without me and went home.

On Tuesday, I returned very early, coffee and breakfast in hand. I asked at the nurses' desk, "When will the orthopedist be in?"

"Oh, he has already been here and talked to your Mom."

"You do realize, she has dementia?"

She looked down at her notes, a blank look on her face. I marched away. We waited all day for physical therapy, which the doctor said she had to have. They said they couldn't come until the tech for the brace showed up. I was beginning to panic about not getting on that plane. I called Hawthorne Ridge and told them to send their evaluator, Keith. I was bringing Mom back. To hell with the hospital and the fact that no one seemed to know what was going on.  Hawthorne Ridge said they would send Keith Tuesday afternoon.

I gave the head nurse the news. Her abrupt reply was, "We will send your Mother's social worker to talk with you."

I waited an hour. The social worker assigned as Mom's advocate finally sauntered in.

"What seems to be the problem? The nurses say you are taking your Mom home today?"

"That's right.  I have already talked to Hawthorne Ridge. They are sending their evaluator over this afternoon. Once he gives the okay, I am moving Mom back to her home."

"But the orthopedist says she has to wear her brace for a month."

"So far she hasn't worn it for two days because your physical therapists can't figure out how to put it back on her. Mom has been lying down since Sunday. The only time she is allowed out of bed, even though she is fully capable of movement, is when she needs to use the bathroom. Then, by the orthopedist's orders, she requires a nurse to help her walk to the bathroom. Again, she is capable of doing this on her own. It has been two days and she hasn't been allowed to move. How can you tell me this is good for her?"

She didn't have a response.

Keith, Hawthorne Ridge's evaluator in my opinion had an air of superiority. Before he even talked to me, he stopped and spoke with the nurses. Then he walked toward me and with a deep sigh and a gruff voice, he began his interrogation.

"The nurses claim that you insist on taking your Mom out of here even though the doctor has not released her."

I pleaded my case. "It was explained to me on Sunday, in the Emergency Room, that Mom would only wear the brace over night. No one mentioned an extended time period. I never would have agreed to that."

"The doctor claims she needs the brace as a precaution."

"Yes, but only for one night. She has not had the brace on since Monday morning and has not moved out of bed." I repeated my question to Keith; "How can you tell me that lying in bed is good for her?"

I looked down the hallway and watched as the nurses and physical therapists glanced away from my accusing gaze.

After watching my mother get out of bed, walk to a chair and sit in it, then stand back up, Keith walked away without much comment. He stopped at the nurses' desk. He conferred with them and once again left me out of the conversation. As he walked away the nurses all glanced my way and I knew the outcome for Mom was not good. I also knew in my heart I was not getting on a plane Thursday.

Immediately, the social worker returned.

"According to Keith's judgment, your Mom cannot return to Hawthorne Ridge. She is no longer independent enough."

"I see," I said, my voice quivering. "What are her options?"

"Well, your Mom doesn't qualify for nursing home care, she doesn't qualify for any sort of intermediate care, and she can't stay here at the hospital, either."

"I'm sorry, I don't understand. So where can she go?"

"That's the problem. Your Mom falls into a grey area. There really is no place for her. Can she go to your home?"

I know the social worker could see the look of shock and disbelief on my face.

"No, she can't come to my house; she can't get up the stairs to the bedrooms and bathroom with that brace on."

The social worker did not answer. It didn't make sense to me that the hospital insisted Mom not leave without the brace, yet they wanted her to go to my home where she would have to climb stairs. It was physically impossible while she wore the brace. I dismissed her with, "I'm sorry, you will have to give me some time to think about this."

Up until this point, I believed I could handle the situation. I had not asked any of my siblings for help. Rocky had offered several times but I refused to let her consider it.  It was her daughter's first parents' weekend at college, a two-day event filled with fun and festivities. Paul was also busy at work with a huge client presentation. Over the week, I grew less confident in my ability to manage the matter alone.

After the visits from Keith and the social worker, I knew I was going to lose it; my patience with the incompetence and lack of caring among the staff reached its limit.

I called Paul at work. "You have to come help me."

"I will be there as soon as my meeting concludes."

Something had to be done so I moved forward. I demanded to see the orthopedist who had not bothered to talk with me, Mom's legal guardian, even though I had explained discussing medical issues with my mother was comparable to trying to talk with a five year old. The doctor was not happy as he marched in with his contingent of interns trailing behind him. I stood and faced him, swallowed, and asked my guardian angel to help me speak clearly.

"Doctor, I understand your concern for my mother's hip, after all that is your job. But my job is to look after the whole person. So far Mom has been in bed 3 days. I know that can't be good for her. You keep stating she needs to wear the brace as a precaution, but if the brace prevents her from moving around you, as a doctor, must realize, that is even more detrimental then the chance of her hip popping back out. Mom needs to return to her home, and she wants to go. I am looking out for the total welfare of my mother, not just her hip."

He glared at me. "Do you accept full responsibility for removing her from here without the brace?"

"Yes."

He turned and walked away while scribbling on his notepad. Later the social worker returned. She said, "The doctor agreed to your terms. Every patient should have someone to speak for them as you did."

This was the first positive acknowledgement I had received, yet, I left the hospital in frustration with tears falling from my face.

I spoke with Paul that night. Even though we both knew having Mom try to live with us again would never work, we felt trapped. We understood the way the system worked. Once a resident moves from a facility, their room is given very quickly to the next in line on a waiting list. Getting Mom back into any home would be difficult, but especially one of our choice. I expressed my concerns, "I guess we have no alternative once the hospital releases her she will not have anywhere else to go. I will have to bring Mom home. I don't know what else to do."

"I think if we take her out of the hospital she will end up living with us because we will not be able to find her another home. Let's call her lawyer tomorrow."

In the meantime, we sent the following email to Hawthorne's director:

Dear Sam,

I am writing out of desperation with regards
to my mother, Ruthanna.
As you are probably aware she dislocated
her hip on Sunday and was
transported to the hospital. I was out of
town that morning but I am
grateful for the professionalism and
response on the part of Hawthorne Ridge to
get her medical attention and arrange for
transportation.

I spent Sunday with her in the Emergency
Room and Corki's hip was "popped"
back in on Sunday evening. She has been
pain-free since. She was admitted
Sunday night for observation with an
orthotic to immobilize her

hip as a precaution. That is my understanding. She is resting comfortably and has been evaluated by the physical therapist and the orthopedist. The hospital has informed me that she will be discharged on Wednesday and is not eligible for acute care, sub-acute care or a nursing home.

I am trying to find the next step in Mom's care that is the best for her. As you know with dementia patients most settings present a real challenge. Even if eligible for care in other facilities, it is my feeling along with several others' that most of these other settings will not be good options either physically or mentally.

I have consulted with many of the doctors including Dr. Keith Cee (her personal physician), Dr. Tiet (her attending

at the hospital), the

Orthopedist, and the physical therapist.

After listening to all the input

and a view of Mom's total care needs (not

just her hip) I am more convinced

than ever that her best option and the best

possible place for her is

Hawthorne Ridge. Keith, (from Hawthorne

Ridge) visited today and we

discussed Mom's situation. My

understanding is he recommended that

Mom not

be re-admitted to Hawthorne Ridge at this

point because of the precautionary

use of the orthotic. Keith did observe her

get up on her own out of chair,

walk on her own and sit back down without

the orthotic. She did this as well

as she usually walks. My understanding is

Keith did not discuss Mom's case

with either physician. She is not in any pain, nor was she in pain when walking. She has worn the orthotic very little for the past forty-eight hours. She has essentially only had it on when being evaluated. She goes to the bathroom on her own without the orthotic. It is not practical for her.

It is my understanding that the orthotic is a precautionary recommendation and not a standing order. She is being re-evaluated by the Physical Therapist on Wednesday.

I feel strongly that Mom's best option is Hawthorne Ridge at this point. My house is full of stairs and would be a danger to her.

I am very adamant in asking you and Dr. Thom, Hawthorne's in-house physician to

reconsider this decision and discuss this situation with Mom's physicians. I believe we all need to look at the whole picture and consider what is best for Mom. I also believe after a better understanding of Mom's situation from her doctors that we can get her back to Hawthorne Ridge. I believe acute or sub-acute care and the lack of attention and unfamiliarity in these facilities will set Mom back mentally and physically. Those options will hinder rather than help
her recovery.

I am her healthcare proxy and strongly believe this is the best course of
action.

I am willing to release Hawthorne Ridge and the doctors from any
complications or issues based on re-admission to Hawthorne Ridge.

If required, I will provide extra help and
care via myself or aides to
smooth any transition.

If the Doctors strongly advise and issue
orders for rehabilitative care
then I see no other options. If, on the other
hand, we are dealing with the
best medical opinions and we are in the
gray areas and mostly being
precautionary, then I feel strongly we
should err on the side of what best
suits Ruthanna. That is Hawthorne Ridge.

We need to understand our options today
and as soon as possible so we can
make arrangements. I sincerely hope you
can confer with the doctors, look at
Ruthanna's needs beyond her hip, and
reconsider your decision based on this

additional input and direct discussion with
her physicians.


Sincerely,


Rosemary Christle-Renaud


It was Wednesday; my flight would probably leave
without me the next day. Mom's lawyer agreed with Paul
and explained under no circumstances were we to take
Mom home with us as she would not be safe at our house.
Paul and I arrived back at the hospital mid-morning. We
asked to speak with the social worker. Two of them
showed up at the meeting. I had told Paul he would have
to do the talking as I had lost all patience and saw the staff
as my enemy. Using his excellent negotiating skills, Paul
persuaded the staff to hold onto Mom for twenty-four
more hours. Then he convinced the director of Hawthorne
Ridge to give Mom and us another chance and to meet
and plead our case. The director said he could meet with
us on Thursday morning. If all went according to plan, Paul

and I could still make a plane to Purdue on Friday. Arriving late was better than nothing. I called Rocky and had her switch our flights.

We contacted our family and friends who were meeting us at Purdue. "Go ahead without us, we will meet you at Harry's Chocolate Shop on Friday."

Thursday morning we walked into the director's office for our meeting. Included from Hawthorne Ridge were the head nurse and the evaluator, Keith. We explained the whole set of circumstances. I said I had agreed to take full responsibility for Mom. To my relief, the director, against the wishes of the evaluator, agreed to let Mom back into her home under the following conditions: her private physical therapist would have to come every day and help her dress and make sure she was getting exercise and Mom would be re-evaluated in one month. I agreed to the terms.

Paul and I walked out of the meeting feeling more confident than we had twelve hours before, but, I was so worn out I found it difficult to find any euphoria.

We returned to the hospital one last time and moved Mom out very quickly. She was a mess. She had not bathed or truly been out of bed since Sunday. The staff at Hawthorne Ridge welcomed her back with kisses and hugs. They made her a cup of coffee, fed her dinner and promised her a nice hot bath in the whirlpool tub.

They took one look at me and sent me home. "Get some rest."

I could only cry in gratitude.

Our flight took off twenty-four hours behind schedule. Upon arrival, I hugged my daughters to me tightly and wept. I almost missed the comfort of wrapping my arms around them, relishing their company and delighting in the sound of their laughter. However, I struggled to fully enjoy the fun, camaraderie and youth filled energy that radiates from Purdue University on a football weekend. I was numb from my hospital nightmare and couldn't find joy. It lay dormant underneath the icy impersonal care Mom and I received.

## Mom's Final Home

During my return flight, I recalled a conversation I had with a Hawthorne Ridge staff member as Paul and I hurried to the exit doors hoping to put our hospital nightmare out of our minds. One of the Earth Angels, who worked there, one with whom I had especially bonded, approached me. She whispered confidentially:

> I'm not telling you what to do, but I went through this with my mother. You need to start thinking of another place for your mom, one where they can take better care of her, give her the nursing skills she needs. Don't wait for another hospital visit because then your mom will not be able to return here and she will end up in a nursing home that you don't approve of.

I thanked her for her advice and gave her a hug. I understood and knew what she was saying to be true: It was time to move Mom from assisted living to a skilled nursing residence.

Upon my arrival home, I called Rocky. Once again, she stepped up as we made plans for another few days of emotional turmoil in finding our mother's final home.

One day, before Rocky could fly up, I visited Mom. I was sitting in the kitchen with her having coffee, when my Earth Angel walked in. I was wondering where my Mom's friend was and I asked her, "I haven't seen Peggy. Is she okay?"

"Oh, that's right, you don't know. She moved to Eddy Village Green while your mom was in the hospital. Now that is the place your mom should be next. Have you seen the houses? The staff just took a tour; we all agree the place is amazing."

When I returned home, I went online to research this new residence. Eddy Village Green (EVG) was a new concept in nursing homes. Instead of one large building, perhaps consisting of several floors filled with hospital-like rooms, EVG consisted of sixteen individual ranch-style homes. Each home has twelve single bedrooms, a family room and one large eat-in kitchen. All meals were prepared by the staff in the kitchen. Together, residents and staff sat down to eat. The homes were built on a single campus. The weekend Rocky had chosen to help m, EVG had an open house in one of the newly built homes. Before even consulting Rocky, I called and put our names on the list of attendees.

The more Rocky and I perused the EVG website, they more we liked what we saw. The other good news was that the nursing home was affiliated with Hawthorne Ridge; it would be an easy move for Mom, a top priority.

Rocky and I knew we had to do our due diligence and spend time visiting other facilities first.

The first nursing home was a drive-by; I never took my foot off the accelerator. The next was a nice brick institutional looking building. It was clean and for the most part the residents seemed happy. But we were overwhelmed with the enormity of the building and the fact that if we could get lost then surely Mom would. She was used to her present home where all hallways lead to the kitchen and living room, preventing the residents from going astray.

As we drove onto the campus of EVG for the open house, we were immediately impressed. We saw several of the ranch homes in different states of construction. They were decked out in the natural colors of the Adirondacks such as sky blue, leaf green and browns of tree bark. When we entered the home set up for the tour, we were excited to see a screened-in front porch and a patio off the rear of the house. The kitchen and family room were open to each other and tastefully decorated. The kitchen table was long and filled the eat-in area; it would obviously accommodate all the residents and then some. A gas fire burned in the corner fireplace of the living room. We gazed through the huge windows that looked out onto the green grass and fall decorations. With sidewalks throughout the community, one got the feeling of a suburban neighborhood. Each bedroom in the house was large, containing a hospital-like bed, which could be lowered and raised. Residents could bring in their own familiar comforter. Rocky and I anticipated moving many of Mom's favorite items from Hawthorne Ridge.

We noticed tracks on the bedroom ceilings. Those were for the staff to transport a resident to their own bathroom when they could no longer accomplish that task. The private baths were large and completely tiled, with an open shower in one corner, allowing the residents free movement within the room. Although this community had all the requirements needed for a nursing facility, we did not think it felt institutional; we felt wrapped in a neighborhood filled with cozy homes.

Rocky and I knew EVG was the place for Mom. There was one drawback; in order for us to reserve a spot for Mom she would have to live in an old-style nursing home for about a month, maybe two until construction was completed. We found that element of the plan depressing. The old brick building consisted of three stories with nursing stations situated at either end of the hallways. As the new homes were built on the campus the residents moved into them one by one as the old building was slowly dismantled. By the time Mom arrived at her interim home, only one floor of the old building remained.

Our thought was since it was near the holidays Mom could be distracted with the extra visits from family who would be in town. We signed her up. We did not give Hawthorne Ridge the chance to tell us it was time for Mom to move to a true nursing home. We heeded the warning from our Earth Angel and started the transition.

Thanks to the efficiency and cooperation of both facilities, Mom's transfer went very smoothly and Rocky and I were happy to only have to deal with the physical move of her personal belongings. We took comfort in knowing Mom's final residence

would become a home she would love.

## The Strength of Sisters

Finding Mom's new home consisted of many weeks of turmoil on my part. I questioned and second guessed myself on every decision. I was troubled with the thought, Mom would be blind sighted with the move and feel total confusion. I spent many nights throwing the blankets off and on, and kicking the cat so many times he grew frustrated and left for calmer sleeping quarters. Finally, a decision was made and Rocky and I felt satisfied and confident with the new home we had found for Mom. We spent many days arranging for her move, the home she would live in the remainder of her life.

But before that relocation could take place Rocky and I decided to continue with a trip that had been planned many months prior, a vacation to Oregon to visit our sisters Rhonda and Renita. It was a gathering of comfort, relaxation and fun for us. We had been each other's emotional and physical support as we all went through some challenging times in the care of our mother. Deciding what to pack and getting to the airport on time was an effort for me. My thoughts were like a wobbly bowl of Jell-o.

As I waited to board my plane, I contemplated the qualities of the sisters I was going to meet. Rocky had always been there to help me and was by my side for difficult decisions. She had missed important times with her family and cut back on her business to be my main support. She was a whirlwind of efficiency as we made difficult decisions in each chapter of Mom's care. She never hesitated to drop whatever she was doing to listen to me cry, yell or grumble about my life as caretaker.

Rhonda, older than me by almost four years, gave spiritual support to both Rocky and me. She reminded us that we were not alone; we only needed to ask our Angels for help and guidance. She gave us moral support and filled our emotional bank when it began to dwindle from self-doubt or when working against a system that seemed indifferent to our dire needs. Rhonda has multiple myeloma, a terminal cancer. During this time, she had it under control, but every day her job, was to stay healthy. That is why she couldn't travel across the country to help Rocky and me. We did the footwork; she backed us up with love and kind words when we were tired or beaten down with our concerns about Mom.

Renita, a few years older than Rhonda, was the "go-to" sister when we eventually needed help selling Mom's house. She took control and hired workers to fix it up and get it on the market. She found a realtor and handled all of the paperwork. She walked through the red tape of selling a house from out of state. She organized the process so that I had nothing to worry about. She also was my loyal ally, coming to my defense when other siblings questioned my actions.

The week's vacation was for us, but between finding Mom a new place, feeling unsure and guilty about a necessary move and somehow keeping all other aspects of my life in place, I felt overwhelmed. I was not exactly sure what I had even thrown into my suitcase. No matter, I thought, Portland has stores.

It was an early flight and I tried to sleep on the plane, but I was too wound up. I concentrated on taking deep breaths and relaxing. I watched movies though I can't remember what they were. I struggled to move past what was going on at home and live in the moment.

Rocky and I had miraculously arranged for our flights to Portland to arrive within an hour of each other. Not bad since we flew in from Georgia and New York. Ted, Rhonda's son and a senior in high school, invited us to attend the assembly he was in charge of for his school's homecoming. We drove straight there.

I could feel the energy from the young people rushing through the entrance doors as we walked in; strangely, it had a calming effect on me. Ted met us and quickly gave his aunts a hug. Then he went into action. He not only planned the assembly, but also led it. Suddenly he burst into the gym, cordless mike in hand, and started persuading the crowd to go wild. He called to his fellow seniors, "Show us your spirit!" The class stood and roared.

Ted responded with taunting the junior class, "Show them you are better."

Each class in turn shouted back with their pride. The gym became a deafening echo of noise bouncing off of the walls. It was amazing to see Ted in action. I could tell he was in his element and I had no doubt he could fulfill his dream of becoming President of the United States one day.

After our eventful first day, we decided to take a trip to Powell's bookstore, a mainstay in the city. The store is huge. I was glad Rhonda was with me because I knew I could get lost in the many stacks of books as they wound their way through the old warehouse. I love the smell of the new and old books combined with brewing coffee. The atmosphere there invites one to sit and stay. So we did.

One day we spent an afternoon wandering through the orange and reds in the calming Portland Japanese Garden. A hue of stillness encompassed massive ancient trees complemented by the small Japanese plantings. Waterfalls added just enough noise to drown out any outside disturbance. Consequently, I began to feel some tension leave my shoulders.

Rhonda rearranged her medication schedule so that she did not have the highs and lows of coming off her steroids and other physically taxing drugs while we were there. This meant she could enjoy wine with us and, as is our tradition, a glass of Bushmill's Irish Whiskey. Wayne, Rhonda's husband, delighted us nightly with scrumptious meals that he lovingly cooked. And there were always bottles of wine to accompany his culinary creations.

On the third day, we headed to the coast of Oregon to a house Rhonda had rented for us in the town of Oceanside, a small cluster of homes that included one restaurant. Renita was able to leave her job as a realtor behind for a few days and join us. Rhonda was driving and I was riding shotgun. Rhonda drove commenting on the enchanting views. Although I had spent a few days searching for my relaxed mode, I still felt uptight. I was focused only on our goal, of getting to our beach house destination.

At first I kept glancing at the speedometer, *my God other cars are passing us. Doesn't she see this?* It took many miles of curving single lane roads for reality to finally hit me as I stopped worrying about myself and focused on Rhonda. This was her coping mechanism. Every day she woke to cancer. Every day she gave thanks to God and her Angels for one more day of life. Taking Rhonda's lead I silently reflected. *Why not enjoy our time together to its fullest? Look out the windows and see the beauty. Listen to your sisters' chatter and hear the love.* The goal was not to get to our destination; the goal was to enjoy the journey and every moment that was given to us. As I focused on these realizations, I finally began to feel a calmness overtake me.

The coast of Oregon was beautiful. The beach, when the tide was out, was great for walking. Interspersed along the sand were boulders sitting like sentinels guarding all of the treasures a beach holds. Out further in the water were towering rocks. When storms came up the waves beat on them with ferocity, splashing up high in the air and sending spray that looked like a geyser shooting off. It rained a lot of the time we were there, but that was Oregon in the fall. We walked on the beach and I found a whole sand dollar, a sign my Angels were with me, or perhaps just luck. We saw flocks of brown pelicans. They flew in a line; the first bird would swoop down from the grey, sunless sky and skim the surface of the white crashing waves and then every other bird copied the same exact movement. The line rose and dove over the surf in a curvy follow-the-leader. It was mesmerizing to watch. Every time I thought the waves would swallow the birds up, they rose back above the water.

Rhonda needed the help and the security of someone's arm when walking. She was always aware a bump or fall could be detrimental. On our way to the beach, down a slippery, steep road she took my arm. We bent our faces together and laughed conspiringly about how we appeared to the neighbors, four women sharing the same house and how they must be saying, "Oh, look there go the lesbians renting that house. But they seem very nice."

All weekend the four of us kept this funny idea going; we laughed knowingly when we went grocery shopping, when we all climbed into the hot tub, when we went out to dinner to that singular but tantalizing restaurant in town. It was our private joke and we used it until we wore it out, finding humor wherever we could. One afternoon as we sat in the hot tub relaxing, and having a serious discussion, the sun suddenly disappeared and it began to hail, we burst into laughter. Another time we giggled like teenagers when we turned the fact we needed firewood into a sexual joke about needing *wood*.

We laughed, but eventually we got around to crying, too. We cried about the unjustness of our mother's illness. We shed tears over the rift in our family and about wrongs we felt had happened in our childhood. It felt good to understand each other's doubts and fears. Such as the longing for parental love, some felt they had missed out on, or how their birth order in the family hierarchy had hurt them. Yet, in turn, we patted each other on the back realizing, *Yes, I have moved past those times in my life and grown from them.*

Like all Christle family get-togethers, we ate. We brought a carload of food, but felt compelled to stop at the grocery to buy more.  Sitting together at a table filled with our favorite munchies in a room overlooking the ocean gave us familiar warmth and filled our hearts with love.  Every evening we toasted ourselves and our unbreakable sisterhood, with Irish Bushmill's Whiskey. Being with my sisters, I truly felt a soothing in my soul; my mind stopped finding reasons to doubt myself. This time together gave me the strength to know I could return to New York and move Mom to her final residence.

Renita, Rocky, Rhonda, me
October 2009

## The Move from Hawthorne Ridge

Unfortunately, the time with my three sisters ended all too quickly. As I returned home I recognized that late fall was upon upstate New York and its residents. Before I had time to settle in to any sort of routine, Mom's move was upon me. As the days grew shorter, my to-do list multiplied. The good news was that all of the paperwork had been taken care of prior to my trip.

On my first day back, I checked in with the staff of EVG. I learned Mom had been assigned a room in the old nursing facility, near to where her new home was being built. This news meant my last task was to finalize her move.

Mom did well with a routine. It was the unexpected that caused her to become nervous and to act out negatively. It could be as simple as complaining about the new situation or as final as refusing to move from her recliner. Either way, we wanted make the move as positive as possible and with that in mind, Rocky and I decided the best way to handle moving Mom was to involve her in as few of the details as possible.

In the interim, I tried to prepare Mom mentally. I spent several visits discussing the fact that she needed more care than she was getting at Hawthorne Ridge. "Mom, you know how some days you find it too difficult to get dressed?"

"Yes, sometimes I can't figure out what to wear and it hurts to bend down and try to pull my pants on."

"Yes, that's what I thought. In your new home, someone will help you with all of those tasks. They will help find your pajamas, they will help pick out your outfit for the next day, and if your arthritis is bothering you too much they will even help button your shirt."

She nodded an affirmation.

"Mom, the good news is right now they are building you a brand new home. It will be beautiful. You will have your own room and your own bathroom. There is a patio, screened-in porch and a huge kitchen. It is a lot like this place, but fewer residents and the staff will be able to help you more."

I repeated this conversation over the course of several visits. Eventually Mom began to tell my sisters when they called the wonderful news. "I'm moving to a new home and they are building it right now," she always said it with enthusiasm.

Rocky did not want me to have to relocate Mom on my own so she flew in again to help. The final afternoon before moving day Rocky and I went to organize Mom's belongings. Rocky sat in the living room with Mom and entertained her with a movie while I went to her room and packed up some items. I stored some things that Mom would not realize were missing, such as linens, clothing and toiletries. Mom was curious as to what I was doing, but I told her I was cleaning her room. We knew telling Mom she was leaving Hawthorne Ridge was a mistake. We did not want to give Mom the opportunity to panic or refuse to cooperate.

The day of the move Rocky and I told Mom we wanted to take her out to lunch. We took her to her favorite diner. As we walked from her beautiful room at Hawthorne Ridge for the last time I was emotional. I tried not to cry, but the tears crowded my vision as the staff came and hugged us their good-byes. Mom did not fully understand what was going on, but Rocky and I knew we would not see these people again. We had come to appreciate this staff and the wonderful care they gave. Even more than that, we had been enveloped in the warmth and love they showed to their residents and their extended families, guiding us through difficult times in our lives. We knew it was time for Mom to move on and understood this day would come. We knew in our hearts Mom's new home would supply her with the additional and necessary care she needed, but this day was still bittersweet.

While we enjoyed our meal, Paul, who had waited in the wings for us to leave, went to work on moving Mom's recliner and a few key pictures. He also brought the wreath that hung on her door. Mom often commented on how the wreath helped her find her room. Rocky and Paul would move the rest of Mom's belongings later in the day.

At lunch, Rocky and I gently told Mom that this was her moving day. I am not sure she fully understood what was going on and her uneasiness increased as the afternoon progressed. During dessert, my phone rang. It was Paul. As if we were spies on a covert mission he whispered, "Everything's all set. You can bring her over."

I hung up and with a huge smile announced, "Okay, Mom, your room is ready. Should we go check it out?"

As if to stall the whole event she replied, "I think I'll finish my coffee first."

So we waited.

As Mom and her two steadfast daughters pulled into the parking lot, Paul met us and helped Mom out of the car and into a commandeered wheelchair. This was the moment we had been dreading. The entrance, although decorated for fall, was institutional looking. Above the door was a sign that read Ford Building.

"What is this?" Mom asked somewhat indignant.

I began to stumble over my explanation.

"Mom, remember we told you that you were moving. Well, this isn't your final home; this is just for a few weeks until your final home can be built."

"Is this building owned by the Ford family?"

Confused, the three of us looked at each other, and then we understood. In Mom's hometown of Wabash the Ford name belongs to a prominent family who often purchased homes and commercial buildings and rehabilitated them to their original glory. Mom had been friends with and an admirer of this family for years.

"Umm, yes Mom, the Ford family owns this building." I lied.

"Well, that is good. Let's check it out."

And, that easily, the moment we had feared, was over. Mom was happy to have found comfort in a familiar name and believed she was in a good place. We wheeled her through the front doors and down a short hallway to her room. Paul pointed out the wreath on her door and pronounced, "See Corki, this is your room. Here is your wreath."

Mom smiled when she saw her familiar recliner near the window and her pictures on the wall. Even though we noticed a huge difference between the rooms, Mom was content to be sitting again in her comfortable chair. She felt at home. As I hung her clothing in her small closet, Rocky and Paul headed back to Hawthorne Ridge and moved the remainder of Mom's personal possessions. There was no going back, literally and figuratively.

The day progressed rapidly and was filled with business items such as; signing the final papers, reviewing Mom's medical history and making decisions about Mom's eventual final days. We met the staff as one-by-one they came in, introduced themselves, and preformed initial tasks. The nurse took Mom's temperature, her blood pressure and heart rate. A dietician came asking what Mom's favorite foods were and if she had any restrictions. The aides popped their heads in to say hello. It was a very busy day and Mom was exhausted when Rocky returned late in the afternoon. Similar to her first move, we stayed with Mom through dinner and tucked her into bed after the staff had helped her get into her pajamas. I think she was snoring as we walked out of the room.

The first day had gone well and we were pleased. But, as Mom spent more time in her temporary home, she became reclusive. Although the cafeteria was just across the hallway from her room, Mom often refused to leave the comfort of her known environment and I often found her sitting alone with a tray of food. Since the path to the temporary offices was within view of Mom's window, she often people watched in the afternoons. I bought a birdfeeder and put it outside in hope of distracting her from the blaring TV. I encouraged her to walk up and down the halls with me, hoping she would realize it was okay to venture out of her room. But, in reality, there was no advantage to leaving her small space as there was only a cubby-hole area at the end of one hallway. Many of the residents sat here in their wheelchairs watching TV. The staff also tried to coax Mom out to participate in activities, but they had a hard time convincing her. Consequently, I made a point of coming more often trying to persuade Mom to enjoy the events with me.

This two-month wait for Mom's final home was nothing short of an endurance test.

Old nursing home Mom
moved to for a
short time
fall 2009

## Reflections

Along with some of the other residents, Mom and I were sitting in the cafeteria waiting for a Christmas concert. I looked up as a group of young performers from a local high school choral group walked in. They were dressed in holiday colors; the girls in short skirts and tights, the boys wearing Christmas ties. As they entered, they were bunched up together very tightly, tripping on each other. With apprehension on their faces, the students glanced around at our group and covered their mouths as they whispered to each other. In that instant, I understood their feelings. I flashed back to a similar moment in my life and recalled when I was in high school and the joy I felt when I sang with a similar Chorus. We participated in contests and we preformed on stage for different organizations.

During the holidays we made trips to nursing homes. Back then, I, too cringed at the site of old people and wondered, *what was that smell in the room? Was it old food or old bodies decaying?* I called to mind how horrifying I felt to realize that people kept on living even after life had already faded from their faces. At that time, I didn't want to be in that room. But, once we began to sing, their aged expressions would brighten. Their seemingly deaf ears would turn to the music and memories of happier times would flicker across their faces.

As I watched our student performers whisper to each other, I could almost hear their conversations. "Wow, these people are so old and scary looking. They don't have combed hair. Some don't seem to have teeth. That guy is asleep in his wheelchair - I hope he isn't dead."

As I sat in the audience that day no longer youthful, tears crept to my eyes. I knew by the way that they looked at me that I was included in this old people category. *"Wow,"* I thought, *when did I become the old person? Wasn't I just that age yesterday? Wasn't I the girl walking in to sing? How did I get to this sad place and stage with my mother? What is Mom thinking? Does she remember being this young, or even my age?*

Melancholy took hold of me as I thought about where my life was at that point. My children were in college, and so, I was not needed every day. I gave up my substitute teaching to be with Mom. I had so many ideas and paths I intended on taking to restart my life again, but each time I began in earnest another crisis needed to be solved with Mom. In my head, I still felt youthful, but my life carried the burden of a half-century and the struggles that go with it. I began to wonder:

> *If I feel the bias from these young people,*
> *am I doing the same to the residents here?*
> *Did I see them as people? They may not be*
> *able to move around on their own or feed*
> *themselves. Some of them smell. Some days*
> *they didn't brush their teeth or hair. But I'll*
> *bet they could share with anyone who took*
> *the time to listen, the stories of their lives.*

At the end of the recital, the singers came around in groups of three or four with gifts for the residents. One group of girls approached Mom and me with caution. They did not want to get too close but they extended their hands out to deliver the gift. It was a Christmas tree pin that sparkled and Mom loved it. Then, ever so slightly, with a little fear and yet resolve, one young girl asked Mom if she could put the pin on her shirt for her. Mom was delighted. A beautiful smile appeared on her unmade face and her uncombed hair somehow seemed to shine. I told the girls my mother was once a high school teacher. "One of the students' favorites," I proudly added.

Mom looked at me and beamed, she may have blushed. She was proud of her life and wanted the young girls to know of her accomplishments. With the small gesture of putting on the pin and listening to me tell of Mom's life the girls recognized Mom's existence and they made a connection. Perhaps they realized somewhere in all of that oldness was a person, the one I knew and loved.

After so many years, I finally realized the gladness I may have brought to others with my singing. I hoped I had taken time to smile and respond to the elderly people as I performed with my group. Thinking about where my life was that day, I conceded that a touch to the shoulder or a smile, maybe a compliment to Mom's fellow residents, was an acknowledgment of their lives.

I encouraged myself with the thought: *Small gestures can truly make a difference.*

Mom and me
December 2009

Christmas celebration
December 2009

## Final Moving Day

Every time I visited Mom, in the Ford Building, with
anticipation, I observed the four new homes being built.
As I drove by, I brought the car to a crawl. I hoped to be
able to peer in the windows to get an idea of how soon it
would be before they were finished and Mom could move
in. I observed walls going up, cabinets being installed,
lights turning on.

Then one day I heard a rumor.

"Did you hear our Moms are all going to be living
together in the same house? We move in the first week of
January."

Excitedly I penciled in a potential moving date.
Eventually, I got the official word from the staff: moving
day would be January 7, 2010. That day worked great into
my family's schedule. Catlin and Kristen would still be
home from Purdue and along with Paul, they could help

me move Mom one final time. I would not need Rocky to fly up again.

The staff was also excited about the move. They gave instructions: we were to have all personal items packed and ready to go on that morning. The custodial staff would move all of Mom's personal belongings and furniture to her new room and set it up as we instructed. In fact, it was not necessary for a family member to be there since the move would take place during a workday. I knew Mom and I both would feel better if I was there to hold her hand.

The evening before the move, I packed Mom's clothing and personal items. She was concerned.

"Posey, what are you doing?"

"Mom, remember I told you that you would be moving to a brand new place? Well, tomorrow is the day."

Immediately, in response to this conversation, Mom returned to her control mode and for the rest of the evening she told me how to pack and where to put everything. It drove me nuts.

The next morning I arrived at 10 a.m., an early hour for Mom. The staff had her up, dressed and she was sitting in her chair having breakfast. I sipped my coffee while Mom slowly ate her meal and hatched, a familiar term she often used to describe her waking up process (a tradition I continued with my girls and still use today).

As with any move, things do not always go according to plan. The day was bitterly cold. It was decided that instead of marching the new residents down the sidewalk in wheelchairs, like ducks in a row, they would be transported by van. This slowed the progress considerably because more than one house was being moved on that day and the van could only serve one at a time.

Around eleven a.m., Paul and the girls arrived. Shortly before that, all of the residents gathered in the cafeteria to alleviate any confusion on their part. With Mom out of the room, they began to take her family pictures, a map of Lake George and other mementos to her new place. The plan was to have her bedroom all set up and decorated before she even set foot in it, making her final transition that much easier on her.

Because the day was behind schedule, Catlin and Paul both had to leave. Kristen stayed behind and returned to the Ford building just as the nurses were lining all of the residents up for the van ride. Mom was sitting in a wheelchair so we wrapped her winter coat around her and tucked blankets around her legs. Kristen entertained Mom and the others waiting to move. They were intrigued with her stories and funny jokes. Some commented that such a beautiful, tall, thin girl was way too young to be in college. As Kristen pushed Mom's chair onto the lift it began to rise.

Kristen became concerned. "Should I jump off?"

"No," a staff member replied, "just make sure her chair doesn't roll."

Mom was very alert and became anxious. The social worker standing with her clip board checking off names observed this and said to Kristen, "Can you ride the bus over with your grandmother? I think she would appreciate it."

"Sure, I guess."

As the bus pulled away, I noticed a sheepish grin on Kristen's face when she realized she was on a senior citizen's bus. I have to admit this made me laugh. The rest of us walked across a parking lot and arrived before the bus pulled up to the new home. We bustled inside. As each and every resident was wheeled into their new home a call came up from the staff and family members.

"Welcome home!"

I was trying to take pictures as the residents came through the door and lost track of Mom and Kristen. Finally, to the delight of everyone, we saw my daughter's smiling face as she pushed her puzzled grandmother through the entrance, the last to disembark from the van. Mom loved being the center of attention and a huge smile appeared on her face.

There was a flurry of activity as coats were removed and all involved admired the new home. It was beautiful. We smelled fresh coffee brewing and the aroma of just baked cookies. We felt Mom was truly, finally, *home*.

Front of Mom's final home
January 2010

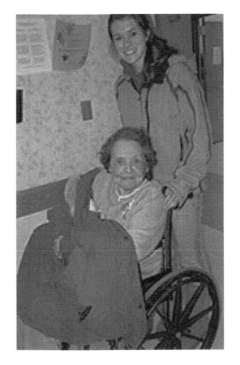

Mom and Kristen waiting to move

Kristen, Paul, Mom

Kristen helping Mom off bus

Mom happy in her new home

Mom and I enjoying the cookies

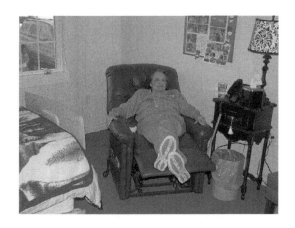

Mom relaxing in her new room

## Decisions

I have made many decisions in my life, some simpler than others. Dessert for example has never been difficult for me; I always ordered anything with chocolate. On a beautiful day, it is always an easier choice to head outside rather than stay indoors and take care of household chores. Saying yes to my husband when he proposed was also a no-brainer. Somewhat more complicated decisions involved buying our current home and letting my children travel overseas to a ski camp.

Other decisions much more difficult to make have had serious ramifications. One of the most emotional decisions involved my mother and her declining health combined with her increasing loss of mental faculties. While living at EVG Mom was well taken care of physically, however, it was obvious even to me, who saw her at least twice a week her quality of life was nil. Her health and mental functions had taken a definite turn downwards. She could no longer control her bowels and bladder. She used a walker and when she tried to sit down she reminded me of an animal trying to find that perfect spot; she would look around the room several times. Finally, she picked out a chair and then stared at it, confused as to how to go about sitting in it. I often had to talk her through the motions.

"Mom, come towards me more. Now turn your back to the seat. No, don't sit down yet, you'll miss the chair."

It was clear she could no longer read. She picked up a newspaper and spent several minutes scanning it. After she put the paper down, I asked he questions about the front page story.

"Mom, did you see this article? I think you used to teach with this man."

"No, I missed that one, what does it say?"

I pretended not to notice and began to read to her only to have her hit the TV remote mid-sentence and the volume came out at an ear blasting decibel.

"Well, I guess we are done reading for today." I muttered sarcastically under my breath.

As I mentioned, Mom's quality of life was not good. She couldn't recall that her husband of over 50 years passed away 10 years before. She had no recollection of her childhood home or the town of Wabash where she spent most of her life. Even the house our family grew up in was lost to her. *What did Mom think about all day?* I wondered.

When I visited I often talked about my siblings or her grandchildren. Frequently, I was met by a blank stare. Sometimes if she was feeling conversational, she would cover her confusion by making general comments, but nothing specific to give away that she did not remember who we were discussing. Other times she looked away, a signal to me she was done with the conversation.

I had come to terms with my mother's dementia although it was still extremely difficult to think about her and not tear up. On the days I visited her, my emotional level was high. Listening to the car radio, I cried over sappy songs. I snapped at my husband for asking me a question more than once. In the grocery line, I lost my patience with people who brought more than fifteen items to the fast lane. On the way to her home, I found myself drumming my fingers on the dashboard following cars, which in my opinion, were driving too slowly. In the middle of a task, if I lost my train of thought, I simply moved onto something else.

I was still somewhat unprepared when I was presented with a new decision while standing in the grocery. When my cell phone rang.

"Rosemary, are you busy?" It was the nurse practitioner from EVG.

"Well, I am in the grocery, but go ahead." I knew if she was calling it was important.

"Remember we had the mobile X-ray unit here when we thought your Mom had pneumonia?"

"Yes."

"The doctor is recommending your Mom go to a hospital for several follow up X-rays."

I pictured the process in my head. I knew what it would take to get Mom into my SUV. We always started with a slow walk as I said, "Mom, we are going out the door in front of us, now turn right. See the big red car? That is mine, walk towards it." "OK, Mom now take a step up onto this stool, turn sideways, no, the other way. Now I am going to help you onto the seat." We had to practically lift her into the SUV, then reach across her to find the seatbelt and to strap her in.

On one occasion, when we took her out for Easter brunch, we could tell she did not enjoy it. She became very confused and worried about where she was. She had a panicky edge to her voice as we pulled up in front of her home. I recalled her saying, "What town are we in? Is this your town, Posey? Well, whose house is this?"

When we did take Mom out, once Paul and I got her back inside, it took awhile for Mom to calm down. The whole day was exhausting.

I told myself on that Easter I would not take her out again unless it was absolutely necessary.

All of these visions raced through my mind as the nurse practitioner waited on the other end. An instant later with the images still vivid, I asked. "What is the problem? What does the doctor think he sees?"

"There are some spots on her lungs, could be a lot of things, but they are recommending a more extensive look."

"What will we do if they find...?"

"Cancer?"

"Yes, cancer."

"You and I both know she is not a candidate for surgery."

"No, and my guess is she is not a candidate for chemo either."

"So I am wondering what we would accomplish then with these X-rays?"

"We might know if she has cancer."

I weighed my answer, but I already knew in my heart what I would say.

"No, I do not want to put her through that. If the only conclusion we come to is to know if she has cancer, or worse, I do not want to put Mom through that."

"I agree, but I needed to discuss this with you."

In a matter of just a few minutes, in the middle of the Asian foods aisle, I made a life-altering decision. I pushed the cart down past the shelves trying to regain my composure; I dropped my list and fumbled picking it up. I determined *I am going to finish grocery shopping first. Then when I get home, I can fall apart. Only then will I let the realization that Mom may have cancer sink into my consciousness.* I shook with this understanding, but I did not falter in my decision.

Though this may seem on the surface a very difficult decision, it was not to me. I had often contemplated this possible situation. I had discussed with some of my siblings how unhappy Mom was, how she was depressed and, of more importance, how her quality of life had dwindled to something I know she did not want. My mother already had a terminal illness: dementia. Dementia always kills. But sometimes the lucky ones die of something else first. I had watched the other residents as their bodies slowly shut down denying their owners any dignity. I wondered if cancer was an answer to my prayers for Mom. Of course, I did not want Mom to suffer in any way. I knew that cancer could be a painful death. But she lived in a skilled nursing facility. She had access to doctors, nurses, pain medication, and Hospice when the time came. *Perhaps*, I thought, *this would be a quicker way for Mom to die, hopefully with less suffering.*

During later visits when I heard Mom cough I worried, but I did not second-guess myself on my decision. I knew if Mom had the capacity to think it through, she would have agreed with me.

## Visits

   As Mom slid further into her dementia, it became increasingly difficult for me to muster the energy to visit her. I never knew how coherent she would be from day to day, interactions became few and far between. Often she sat gazing into space. On those days, I struggled to get her involved in a conversation. Sometimes I tried to draw her into talking with a question, which she might not answer. If she did, it was with one word or the nod of her head. With great effort, I would start over again trying to find another topic. At times, it seemed easier to just sit together and watch a blaring TV. She was okay with that; I think she simply enjoyed me beside her.

   On the days I did visit, I procrastinated about getting there. I tried to set a schedule to arrive late in the morning. It might have been easier to give myself permission to show up when time permitted, but I felt guilty about not truly wanting to go and made myself show up sooner rather than later. Instead of sticking to that schedule however, I sought out chores that suddenly had to be completed before I departed. Usually my distractions took long enough that I did not arrive in time for lunch. I dreaded sitting through meals with Mom and her fellow residents. Lunch could be sickening. Some residents were coherent and could hold conversations; others had to be spoon-fed their blender-pulverized meals. One woman drooled through the entire meal and then would let out a very loud wail just before she burped. It was disturbing and to say the least, not very appetizing.

To appease my guilt I brought Mom a chocolate bar or a dish of ice cream. She loved both. One day I brought ice cream for Mom and me. As I walked in the front door, I found her sitting in her favorite rocking chair in the common room watching the Disney Channel. I handed her a dish of Death by Chocolate and settled in to eat my non-fat creamsicle yogurt. Unexpectedly, one of the other residents let lose a screaming fit directed at me.

"You lousy son of a bitch, where is *my* ice cream!"

I cringed with the shrieking sound of her voice and the barrage of obscenities. She continued unabated for several minutes. She would not let up with her ranting and eventually started in on the staff and anyone else who walked in the room. I found myself thinking: *it is hard enough to come through that front door, now I have to endure this?*

I thanked God Mom had become docile with her dementia, a blessing. She finished her ice cream without taking a breath and remained oblivious to the woman's rant. I, on the other hand, was becoming unglued. When Mom said she needed to go to the bathroom I gladly had one of the staff help her to her room and we stayed there, away from the screamer.

As we sat in her room I struggled for a conversation. On more than one occasion, Mom and I talked about the pictures on her bedroom walls, her grandchildren and great grandchildren. I began my chatter and once again pointed out who each child was and how they related to Mom. I sounded like an old record that was played too many times, becoming worn and thin.

Later, I picked up the newspaper and read some articles aloud to Mom. She did not comment. As the room grew quiet, I reminisced with myself. My mind wandered to past conversations I once had with Mom. At that time, I dreaded to hear her views of the world; they all seemed negative. At that moment, however, I would have been glad to hear her discuss anything. As she sat in her wheelchair and looked out the window; she did not even acknowledge what I was reading. I wondered *will Mom be content if we both just sit here?*

After some time I noticed she was falling asleep. It was approaching her afternoon naptime, so I took this as an excuse to make my exit. Mom liked to doze in her recliner. I began to help her shift to that chair from her wheelchair, but it was a process. I moved the seat of the recliner into a standing position with a remote, which made it easier. Then I instructed Mom on how to stand, turn and sit back in her recliner. Again, I pushed the remote button and the chair went into recline. With her legs up, she settled in for a nap. She did not mind me leaving and, honestly, I was happy to go.

Over the weekend while I was out of town, Mom's friend Peggy passed away. It saddened me to realize her daughter, Margy, would not be around when I visited. I would miss her comfort, her laughter and her kind smile. More importantly, I realized and admitted to myself that parts of me were envious of Margy. I knew when Mom died it would be difficult; I could not fathom the emotions I would go through. Still I questioned, *can it be any more difficult than this day to day waiting?* I realized I was jealous that Margy would no longer have to return to watch the vibrant mother she once knew drift away into a shell. She was finished with the struggle to appear upbeat, when emotionally she was silently screaming. Margy was finished with the years of watching her mother slowly die.

Margy could now move out of the darkness and gloom and begin to remember her mother, as she once was, not as a dementia patient.

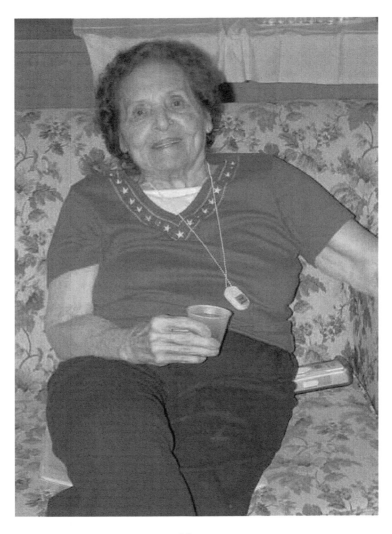

Mom
2010-2012

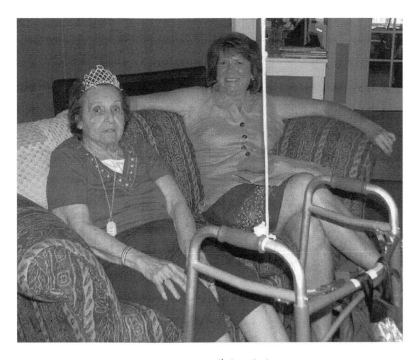

Mom on her 86<sup>th</sup> birthday
July 7, 2010

Easter bonnet Mom and I made
2010-2012

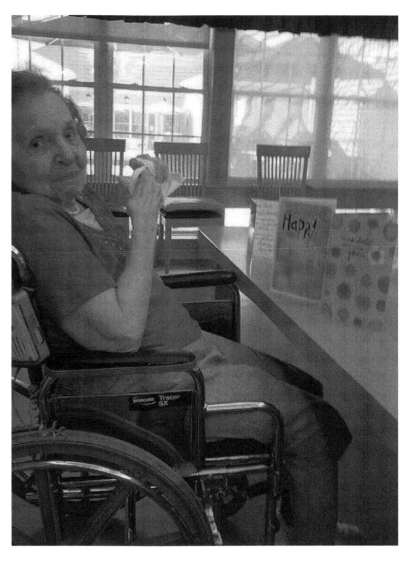

Mom with birthday cards
2010

A birthday martini
2010

## Birthday Thought

"I miss Mom calling me on my birthday. I'm tired of always being sad."

Rocky let her comment drop off with a heavy sigh. I understood what she meant. My days didn't seem to have the same brilliant sunshine they once had either. A few short years before I literally would stop and ask myself, *how did I get to have such a wonderful life?*

Three years after Mom's diagnosis of dementia, I still enjoyed an incredible life. I tried to stay positive, but anything could change my focus and in an instant, I could become tearful over something as simple as a country song. Living with a loved one who had dementia was a slow slide into nothing. Our final good-bye lingered just over my shoulder. A shadow fell across the sunshine in my day.

I knew that on my birthday I would not hear from Dad, I accepted that. He had been gone ten years. There were times, when pursuing an activity I knew he enjoyed, I would think, Dad *would have enjoyed this.*

I did not have that realization with Mom.  She was still alive. The child in me wanted a call from Mom on my birthday. It would have been wonderful to see her in the kitchen baking my favorite cake. It was difficult for my heart to understand what my mind already knew; Mom wouldn't call because she couldn't. Mom didn't remember it was my birthday because Mom didn't remember me. I understood Rocky's sadness.

Even though Mom's brain no longer functioned, her body carried on. We continued to wait.

## Good-bye

I have said many good-byes in my life, some more memorable than others. Before I knew what death truly was I said good-bye to my best friend's father when he died of a heart attack.  He was only forty-two; we were just ten.

Not all good-byes were that shocking. I had three older sisters who, upon their graduations from high school, went away to college. I waved to each one in turn as the car ventured around the corner, out of sight. I saw them infrequently after they left. I had the comfort of knowing they would be there if I needed them, but once they were gone from my small world, it was difficult to include them in my teenage self-absorbed life.

I tearfully said good-bye to my parents and younger siblings when it was my turn to leave for Purdue University. I thought I would miss them all terribly. Once I was at school though, I fell in love with college life and did not look back. I met many different people and found many new friends. Some friendships still continue; others drifted in and out of my life, yet changed my soul in some way.

When I married and moved east to New York State, I left Indiana without a single tear in my eye. I was ready to begin my new life. Once established in our new home, Paul and I reached out to my parents. We still wanted to be a part of their lives. Mom and Dad would make the drive from Indiana and as their visits approached, I couldn't wait to see them and counted the days until their arrival. We always enjoyed their stays. Yet, as their departure date loomed, I knew I would be glad to get back to my normal routine. It was always a bittersweet good-bye.

Sadly, I remember the last time I saw my father. It was almost a decade ago and he lay in a hospital bed. I had been with him and Mom for a week. It appeared he was making a recovery from a heart attack and surgery. I was headed home to my husband and two young daughters. Exhausted, I was ready to leave daily hospital visits, bad cafeteria food and lumpy hotel mattresses behind me. As I hurried out the door to catch a flight home I turned around. I caught my father watching me leave and saw in his eyes his love and his pride in me and the knowledge he would never see me again. He knew and at that moment, I suppose I knew it, too. Still, my only thought was to go home and succumb to the comfort of my husband and daughters. The idea of a final good-bye was too emotional. Dad died a few weeks later. As sad as that was I treasure the time I spent with him while he was in the hospital. I hold in my heart that look I saw on his face when I walked out the door.

Because it took six long years, my good-bye to my mother was even more difficult. It went on, painfully, every day.

In the beginning, when she was still able to vocalize her desires, Mom and I discussed what she wanted. She confided she was ready to move in with me. She told me how she wanted her money spent. She trusted me to follow her wishes. She made it clear that she did not want to go to a traditional nursing home and, as her illness progressed, I worked hard to honor that request. When she moved into Hawthorne Ridge it must have been difficult for her to see others further along in their illness, knowing that was where she was headed.

Once, during her temporary stay in the Ford Building, Mom and I walked past another resident. The woman was propped up in a reclining chair with inadequate blankets covering her nightgown. She was sitting in the middle of the hallway. This shell of a woman was in the last stages of dementia. She could no longer communicate, could not walk, did not eat, and, for the most part, she slept all day awaiting merciful death. The scene was difficult to observe.

"Please do not let that happen to me," Mom said.

I rubbed her back and promised I wouldn't. It was never communicated between us, but we both hoped she would not get to that point, that some illness would take her before she had to linger in that condition. It was heartrending for Mom to realize where her life was headed. As that day approached, I hoped she would no longer comprehend her situation. It grieved me to be with Mom. Every visit was a reminder that I was saying good-bye to her. I said good-bye when I realized that she could no longer hold a conversation and that it had become more comfortable for her to sit flipping through the television stations. Every time I saw she had wet herself, I said good-bye. I said good-bye when the phone rang to tell me of another illness or that she had fallen. Each farewell was agonizing. I never got used to seeing my strong-willed mother fumble for words or stare into nothing.

I have so many memories of my mother and our life together. Some are comforting, some cut into my soul with their coldness, but that was Mom. She wasn't always warm and fuzzy. Still, I had great love and respect for her. I hope that this dementia patient who resembled my mother would not ruin the lovely memories I had of my mom - the mother I originally said good-bye to when I first drove back to Indiana and found her sitting alone in her dark home in stained clothing, crumbs all around her.

## Final Decision

The Elvis impersonator sang to his crowd of adoring fans. The women swooned when he presented them with a brightly colored scarf and a kiss. One stood to dance with him and he obliged her. Other enthusiasts couldn't stand because they were in wheelchairs. Many did not comprehend his words, but still the music brightened their day.

Mom and I were enjoying the EVG block party. Each of the sixteen houses had a theme in celebration of the day. Because of the sweltering one hundred degree heat, all events had been moved indoors. Where Mom lived, House Three, there was a Saratoga Springs theme. They had a casino set up on the dining table. Earlier, I had arrived in time to observe Mom being prompted to place her chips on numbers and watch the spinning roulette wheel hopefully stop and make her a lucky winner.

"Hey Mom, do you want to go see Elvis perform and then afterwards we can get a root beer float?"

"Yes, I would love a root beer float," she said, haltingly.

The footrests were added to her wheelchair and I began to push her towards the front door. It had probably been a year since Mom last left the familiar comfort of her home at EVG. She either sat on the back patio or the screened-in porch out front to get her fresh air. As we approached the door, Mom had a moment of panic. She grabbed the bench in the foyer and would not let go.

"Are we going out this door?"

"Don't worry, Mom I'll take care of you. Besides you want a root beer float, don't you?"

She nodded her affirmation and slowly released her grip on the bench, letting her hand drag across the seat as I moved her wheelchair forward. The outside air hit us like the heat just released from an open oven, and Mom blinked her eyes to adjust to the sun. We heard the thumping of the bass beat and the lyrics to *Burning Love* as we made our way across the street to House Four, identical to Mom's only reversed in setting and decorated in a different color scheme. Elvis was gyrating his hips causing the large sequined belt that adorned his blue polyester jumpsuit to bounce around seductively. I parked Mom in her wheelchair towards the back of the group and found myself a place to sit. We listened to Elvis croon for almost an hour. As the crowd began to thin I wondered if Mom was getting tired.

"Mom, do you want to head back home?"

She turned to me, a huge smile on her face. "No, I'm having fun. Aren't you?"

I looked around at the many smiling faces. The staff was laughing at the impersonator's jokes and the audience, many with dementia, sat enthralled while the music brought back memories or feelings happier times.

I was awash in mixed emotions, sad that Mom and I rarely communicated anymore, but so happy to see her enjoying herself. Elvis wound down his act. Like many performers I had seen at EVG, he seemed truly disappointed his time was over, leading me to believe his joy came from giving to his audience. Mom and I headed to House Two for our root beer floats and then back home to House Three to top off the afternoon. I got her adjusted in front of the TV and brought her an ice-cold glass of water.

"Mom, I have to leave now."

"Where are you going, I'm not sure if I should be here? What car should I take to get home?"

"Mom, you live here and there is the door to your bedroom. I'm going to the grocery, I'll be right back."

I often said this to her when I left, whether it was true or not, because the statement was something she could relate to and in her mind she knew I would return soon. Within a few minutes of my leaving she would have forgotten I was ever there. As I walked towards the door, I cautioned the staff that Mom was nervous. As I left I noticed Maryanne, one of the staff, come over and put her arm around Mom's shoulders she asked, "Corki, do you need to use the bathroom? Let me help you."

If Mom agreed, I knew Maryanne would not be able to help Mom on her own because it now took two staff members to move her from her wheelchair. Mom, at that time, was supposed to walk from one room to the other, but that had become too difficult. Mom's brain no longer allowed her to remember how to walk, chew or swallow.

Also at this point Mom started to make statements that were incomprehensible. "This isn't Dr. Phil; I thought it was the other guy who is number three," she said one day as we watched his show.

"Hmmm, not sure, Mom." I realized we had entered another phase of her illness.

While I was driving home, my cell phone rang. It was the nurse practitioner from EVG. I had been waiting for her call so I found a quiet street and pulled over. I wanted to discuss a health issue of Mom's that had become serious. Mom had endured reoccurring urinary tract infections for several years due to the fact she had a large kidney stone. The stone couldn't be broken up with shock wave therapy and Mom was not a candidate for surgery. However, the medical staff had recently brought to my attention that

Mom has reached a critical stage with her infections. It was suggested that Mom's past urologist be contacted and further treatments be sought. The urologist requested that Mom be brought into his office, which of course presented problems. The first was that I could not get Mom into my SUV on my own; an ambulatory transport had to be hired. Additional problems were Mom's inability to give a urine sample and she wasn't mentally able to answer any questions. I was also not sure there was anything else that could medically be done for Mom. I actually wondered if having Mom go in was the easiest way for the urologist to protect himself from any malpractice accusations. I requested a call from the nurse practitioner.

"Posey, let me explain where we are with your mother's history on this problem. Going back to my notes last January, she has had several UTIs that were fought with eight different types of antibiotics. Your Mom's symptoms disappear, but the infection was truly never wiped completely out. Over the past several months, the bacterium continued to mutate and now can only be treated with two types of antibiotics, one being an intravenous drug. What needs to happen is that the staff has to stop thinking that your Mom has developed another UTI. They must understand that she continually has an infection, because the kidney stone is infected. Our course of action needs to wait until your Mom actually has a fever, instead of observing her other symptoms which are disorientation, lack of appetite, listlessness."

"Yes, I agree, we all know these are her first symptoms whenever her UTI becomes worse."

"Understand that eventually this bacterium will continue to mutate to an infection we can't fight with antibiotics. More than likely, this is what will kill your mother."

There was silence on the phone because I could not think of any words to utter.

She continued, "Today I spent time with your mother and I think you realize, as I have been observing, that she has been declining this year."

"I agree."

"She is fading. She needs to be prompted to play bingo and she doesn't hold conversations. She has days where she forgets how to eat and, as you know, she prefers her wheelchair as walking has become too difficult. She really doesn't have much to live for."

Even though I knew all of these conditions were true, I still found it difficult to talk over the lump forming in my throat. I tried not to cry. Somehow, I found my voice and threw in a comment. "Two years ago the urologist told me that there was not a lot we could do for Mom to get rid of the stone, but it was not causing her any pain."

"Posey, you have always been a great advocate for your mother. You have always put her comfort and what is best for her first. But, I do not want you to second guess yourself at your mother's death. If you feel you should take her in to see the urologist one last time, to make sure there are no other options, for your sake or perhaps so that none of your siblings second guess you, then you should do it. You should know that I am perfectly fine with no visit to the urologist. Whatever your decision, you need to be strong about it and have no regrets."

I couldn't answer. The lump that had formed in my throat had grown with each kind word she said and my eyes clouded as tears rolled down my face. She had pried open my heart spilling out my carefully guarded emotions. I felt validated to have a health care professional commend my care for Mom and I finally whispered a choked, "Thank you."

To be honest, I prayed for over a year that Mom did not get to the stage of dementia where she had to be spoon-fed and lost all coherent thought. I recalled our conversation after we saw the woman in her last stages of dementia and my promise to Mom on that day: I would not let her lose her dignity.

I stuck to my words.

## Brink of Death

In October, while visiting my sister Rhonda, she invited me to go with her to an Angel reading. I wasn't sure exactly what this entailed, but I had followed her guidance on spirituality before so I decided to give this new idea a try.

We met in a small room, at a local library near Rhonda's home in Portland, Oregon. The Angel reading consisted of tarot-like cards read by a confident, soft-spoken woman. She radiated a feeling of calm and I liked her.

"Rosemary, a project you are working on will be ending in January."

"Do you mean the book I am writing? Or are you referring to my mother?"

"I'm not sure, maybe both."

*Interesting,* I thought as we said our good-byes to the others who had gathered with us. Inspired, I decided that upon my return home I would get busy finishing the details of this book. I did not give the Angel Reading another thought.

But, on January 1, 2012, the Angel reading warning about my "project" came into full light. A group of us had just watched as Paul and some crazy friends plunged into the frigid waters of Lake George. We were walking into Judd's Bar in the village for our traditional beer and chicken wing feast when my phone rang.

"Rosemary, this is Carol the RN from Eddy Village Green. Just wanted to give you a heads up. Your Mom is not doing well. She didn't eat lunch and we are putting her to bed. No need to come in, but I thought you would like to know."

"Okay, thanks. I will be in later this afternoon."

I felt an icy slice of dread slide through my body as if I had jumped into the winter lake myself. *Oh my God, it is January first, did the Angel reading mean this? Is Mom the "project" that will end in January?*

I walked inside the warm bar to the smiles and concern of my friends.

"Everything alright?"

"Mom is not doing well, but she is okay for now."

Since these were very close friends, I did not feel vulnerable when I confided to them the Angel Tarot Card reading and this new immediate feeling of dread. I braced myself for what would become a rollercoaster ride that would take me on emotional highs and lows for the next fourteen days.

On Monday, the nurse practitioner from EVG called and said she had examined Mom and felt she had pneumonia. She wasn't going to wait for an X-ray; she started her on Levaquin, an antibiotic, and oxygen with nebulizer breathing treatments four times a day. I called Rocky and gave her the news. I knew if Mom continued to get worse, she would fly up to be with both of us.

I spent the morning with Mom on Tuesday, but around dinnertime Carol called and said Mom was having difficulty breathing and seemed distressed. She wanted to know if she could start her on morphine. The pain medication would help calm Mom and give her some comfort.  I gave permission, but with a feeling of foreboding, Paul and I packed books and phone chargers as we headed out the door to be with Mom. We wanted to be prepared.

On our arrival, I noticed several of the staff members were looking very worried as we entered the building. Jan, an aide, and Carol came over and hugged me.

Jan said, "I put a fresh pot of coffee on for you; I'll bring it in when it is ready."

Another aide was sitting with Mom, watching her, when we walked into her room. He got up and left with a nod in our direction. Mom lay in her bed. Her entire upper body moved up and down as she labored to breathe in and out. She looked yellow and gray at the same time. Her muscles jumped and her jaw was tight; I saw fear in her dementia-lost eyes. Our coffee arrived on a silver tray with ceramic mugs. Most of the residents use lighter weight plastic mugs that are easier for them to pick up. The ceramic mugs and coffee service were a supportive gesture from the staff to let us know their hearts were with Mom and us. It was not lost on me.

I pulled a chair up to Mom's bed and took her hand. Another chair was brought in for Paul. Mom's hand was clammy and she did not register my presence. Carol hovered over all three of us.

"The morphine should start working soon. It will take the edge off of her anxiety and allow her to be more comfortable and hopefully she will begin to breathe easier."

Paul and I nodded our acknowledgement and, as we sat there with Mom, her breathing did become easier. I called my daughters, who were together for dinner, to let them know where we were. They decided to check on their Grammy Cork and to bring Paul and me some sandwiches. By the time Catlin and Kristen arrived, I was high on late evening caffeine and starving. Mom was much more comfortable and the girls sat with her while Paul and I ate our cold sandwich and potato chip dinner. After a few anxious hours, I felt Mom had come through this day of crisis and we all went home. I called Rocky and gave her an update.

"Should I come up?"

"Not yet. Let me see how she is doing tomorrow."

On Wednesday, I went to sit with Mom. She looked bad. There was no improvement. I sat with her and cried. Then I made my call.

"Rocky, I can't tell you how things are going to go, but I have a feeling..."

I choked on my next words and she finished for me.

"You need me to come?"

"Yes."

I sputtered out my reply through the ache in my throat from trying to stifle the dread and sorrow I felt. Not so much for Mom, she seemed comfortable, but for Rocky and me, and what I expected we would go through over the next few days. I felt guilty about pulling Rocky away from her family and her life yet I knew she would not want me to go through this alone. She had made me promise I would call.

Thursday I got up early and started working on accomplishing all of those tasks that needed to be done before I could get to Mom. As I was walking into the grocery my phone rang. It was Lynn, the nurse practitioner.

Posey, are you busy? Can you talk?"

"I'm in a parking lot. Wait, I'll sit in my car."

"Actually, can you come to your Mom's house? I am here now and I will wait for you."

I did not know what Lynn wanted to tell me. I was grateful my fingers pushed the buttons the day before to call Rocky. I whispered a silent prayer of thanks to my Angels.

At that moment, Rocky was on a plane coming to my rescue.

I found Lynn in the nurses' office and we sat down together.

"Posey, it doesn't look good. The X-ray shows pneumonia in her left lobe, but I also hear congestion in her right lobe, perhaps suggesting heart failure. Your Mom is frail, she is tired."

As tears began to roll down my cheeks, I asked, "Are you saying I should call my family?"

"I can't say exactly how this will work out, but many times people in your Mom's condition do not recover from pneumonia like this. I am increasing the Levaquin dosage. Yes, call your family."

We both stood and Lynn gave me a hug of understanding. As we walked out into the living room, Jan asked if I wanted coffee.

"I, um, I don't know."

"Take some coffee, Posey," Linda kindly chided. I drank my coffee and wrote the notes I would need to send an email out to my sisters and brother.

That evening Paul picked Rocky up at the airport and she arrived just in time for a family birthday celebration for Catlin. We had decided to continue with the party because we weren't sure we would get another opportunity to all be together for awhile. Kristen was returning to Purdue on Saturday. That evening we drank wine and ate lobster,

Catlin's favorite meal. We laughed over old familiar stories ignoring the sadness welling up inside each of us.

Before Kristen left for school, she spent Friday afternoon with her Grammy Cork. At that time, no one knew the outcome of Mom's illness, but it was apparent that whatever happened, this was probably Kristen's last chance for a good-bye with her grandmother. Rocky and I walked out of the room to allow her some time alone to say her farewell.

I can't tell you what happened specifically on any of the next several days. As Rocky said, each day was like the horror version of the movie, *Groundhog Day,* because every moment was a repeat of the day before. It was difficult watching our mother struggle to breathe and waiting to see if the drugs would stop the infection. Because of her dementia, Mom no longer communicated so we took educated guesses. If Mom began to squirm more in her bed or seemed uncomfortable in any way, we asked for more morphine. Rocky and I prayed for guidance. We prayed for signs. We talked with Rhonda and asked her if she was getting any feelings or word from her Angels.

Rocky recalled being with our Dad in his last few days; she felt we needed to let Mom know it was okay for her to move out of this world.

Coffee service
January 2012

## Will You Help Me Pass?

Because of Rocky's suggestion, whenever we entered Mom's room one of us would hold Mom's hand as she slept and whisper or silently meditate with her. One afternoon as I sat alone with her, with the lights dimmed, I began to silently convey to Mom: *Mom it is okay for you to pass. Your husband is waiting for you. Your beloved brother, Odie, your sisters Maxine and Betty, Uncle Bob, and your mom and dad, all are waiting for you.*

I asked all of her deceased loved ones, *Help Mom cross over to Heaven or the afterlife.* I prayed to Michael the Archangel, *gather her family members who have passed. Lead them; help them reach out to Mom and bring her back with them. Please make her passing easy; don't let her struggle for breath. Let her die peacefully.*

I silently told Mom, *We have been on this journey together, but it is time for it to end. I will be here with you, but you need to go be with Dad and the others.*

I was anxious and upset, questioning the recent choice of putting Mom in the care of hospice, ending any further use of Levaquin once this dose was completed. During my rollercoaster of a week, I had asked the Angels and Michael the Archangel to help me with my decision.

For a long time I continued to hold her unresponsive hand.

Finally, I grew tired so I moved to a more comfortable chair. My cell phone rang; it was Paul so I answered it. As soon as I spoke, Mom recognized my voice. She stirred and looked at me questionably. She spoke in a full sentence, something she hadn't done in months, but I didn't understand what she was trying to say.

"Wait, hold on Paul," I said. I moved closer to Mom and then her sentence became startlingly clear.

"Will you help me pass?"

Stunned, I fumbled and dropped my phone. I took her hand.

"Yes, yes, Mom that is why I am here. I have been on this journey with you and I will be here until the end. I will help you. Dad is waiting; your family is waiting. It is okay for you to go."

She closed her eyes and went back to sleep. I sat with her holding her hand, watching her breathe. I was sobbing as I felt a great relief wash over me. I had asked for a definitive sign and I shivered with the realization my prayer had been answered.

To this day I still find it difficult to believe Mom's verbal request; it all seems surreal to me. I remind myself that whether I misunderstood my mother or not, at that instant her communication with me was the sign I was seeking.

Amazingly, Mom slowly, painfully, crawled from her brink of death and recovered. The antibiotics worked. On the recommendation of the nurse practitioner, we continued with hospice. As a family, we decided to not prolong the inevitable. We came to terms with Mom's terminal disease, dementia. Her quality of life had diminished to where she could only eat pureed food and she struggled to swallow liquids that were the thickness of honey. She was still on oxygen and the nebulizer treatments. Mom could not eat her beloved chocolates. She couldn't follow a conversation or TV program any longer. Many days she did not recognize us.

Before her dementia, Mom had a conversation with several of her children. She also wrote letters of intent about her care. We as a family followed as much as possible the directives Mom put forth and we felt our decisions about hospice respected her wishes, and I was able to fulfill her final plea to me.

In the end, I did as Mom asked. When it was time, I helped her pass.

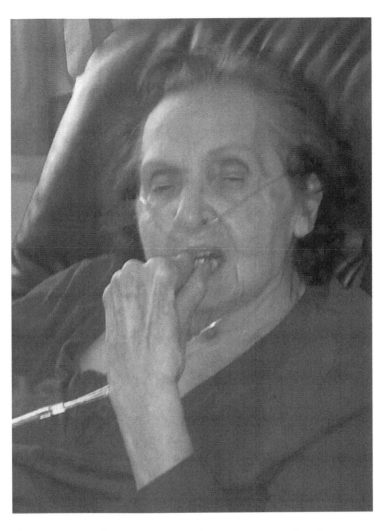

Mom after recovering from her near death
January/February 2012

## A Time to Die

I took my mother's long slender fingers and cupped them between my hands, which were remarkably similar to hers. I noticed this as I held her hand and stroked it as I said good-bye, after she had taken her last breath. I wondered, *why had I never noticed her fingers before? What else had I missed?* It was too late now; my mother was dead. It was Tuesday, February 21, 2012; the eleven-year anniversary of my father's passing. I felt his presence in the room with me all day and I knew he had come to take her with him.

I cried with relief, sadness and gratitude. Relief that her six year slide into nothing was over; sadness because this was my mother and that covered a whole myriad of thoughts and memories on my part; gratitude that my mother was now free once again to use her incredible brain.

The Friday before Mom passed; she and I sat in the family room at EVG and watched the comings and goings of the other residents. She looked so good and happy that I took her picture and sent it to my siblings. Her appearance seemed odd since just a few weeks before she had come so close to death. Feeling relaxed about Mom, I enjoyed that weekend with friends in the Adirondacks skiing and laughing.

Yet, on Monday, as I was having breakfast with a friend, the nurse from EVG called. She said Mom had taken a turn for the worse and I should come in. As I walked into Mom's room, I saw the look of panic on her face. She was scared and struggled to breathe. The nurse was talking about antibiotics and, for a moment, not truly paying attention I nodded in agreement. She left just as I came to my senses. I called hospice and confirmed with them our family plan: no more antibiotics. We decided we did not want a repeat of the recent events and to draw out the ending we all knew was coming.

I sat with Mom, held her hand and promised I would be with her. I watched as the morphine began to take hold and she lost the look of fright in her eyes. By mid-afternoon Mom was sleeping. Remembering the last vigil, I decided now was a good time to accomplish all of the work that I knew needed to be completed before I could return and sit the extended hours or days it took for Mom to pass. Hospice informed me that the next twenty-four hours would determine how long she would linger.

I also needed to call Rocky and give her the alert. I knew she was on vacation and I didn't want to destroy that until absolutely necessary. Instead, I called her husband, Scott. I told him to be ready to make flight decisions, but at that point I wasn't sure of anything.

That afternoon, after a hurried accomplishment of my tasks, my friend Janine volunteered to bravely be my companion and returned to EVG with me. Mom was awake and fairly alert. Janine and I both saw the panic in her face. I requested more frequent doses of morphine. I wanted her to be comfortable. We sat with Mom. I held her hand and repeated my mantra of encouragement giving her permission to leave this life. She fell asleep and as Janine and I went home to get some rest, my thoughts returned to the fourteen day ordeal Rocky and I endured in January. I fully expected Mom to linger a few more days. I shuddered.

That night, much to my surprise, I slept soundly. I awoke early with the knowledge I would get a call very soon to come check on Mom. At seven-thirty a.m. the call came and by eight-thirty I was back at Mom's bedside.

Upon walking into her room, I sensed a change. Mom looked much worse. She was very incoherent. I knew today would be a long one and although I tried not to recognize it, I somehow felt this was the end. At ten a.m. hospice dropped by. I don't think they were prepared for Mom's sudden turn for the worse. As the hospice volunteer walked into the room I asked, "Do you have any idea of how much longer Mom will be with us?"

She hesitated. "I'm assuming you had a chance to read the small booklet you received from us?"

I nodded; I had read it several times.

"Remember, the book gives some definitive signs for death and it looks like your mom has some early ones. But each person dies in their own way. I can't be sure."

She stayed with me awhile but soon I wanted to be left alone. Our conversation dwindled and eventually she walked out. Using some of the knowledge I had read in the hospice booklet, with some trepidation, I pulled the blankets from Mom's hands and feet. They were turning blue; a sign the end was coming.

The nurse practitioner called me into a private room. "This is it; she will not pull through this time."

Lynn, who had become my friend, was worried about me. She insisted someone be with me.

"Where is Rocky? Have you called her yet?"

"No, I will now but Lynn, my husband Paul is coming soon. I will not be alone."

As I left her office, I called Rocky. Scott had already prepared for her departure.

"You better come, this is it."

Before making her preparations to fly up to be with Mom and me, Rocky put out an alert to all of our siblings.

That day I sat with Mom. With a lump in my throat, I read her the poems she had recited to us as children. I sang to her the songs we enjoyed around the campfire. I held her hand. I promised her that her children would all be fine, that she had done her job and it was okay for her to leave.

The staff was upset. They had been through this before and knew what was coming. Many came in as their shifts were ending. I stood to one side as they each took Mom's hand and said their good-byes. I cried. Even in her demented state Mom had touched their lives. Along with Lynn the staff also worried about me. They fretted over me bringing me lunch.  They kept a fresh pot of coffee brewing. Lynn stopped by two to three times that day, mostly to check on me. I never felt alone. I gained comfort from the staff, Mom's extended family.

At one point, I was in Mom's bathroom getting a wet cloth for her forehead. She was burning up with fever. With my back to the room, I felt a man's presence. *Paul must be here,* I thought as I turned around, but the room was empty. I returned to my chair and sat beside Mom. I began to sing to her. As I stumbled over the words, desperately trying not to completely fall apart, I felt my father standing behind me, keeping vigil with me. I touched my shoulder where I felt his hand. Even though it appeared it was only Mom and me in the room, I knew we were not alone.

Paul arrived and we sat together for the remainder of the day and evening. It was Mardi Gras and the staff insisted we eat. They brought us the most delicious seafood gumbo for dinner. Later, during one of their frequent checks, they interrupted the party they were throwing for the residents to change Mom and make her more comfortable. They wept as they preformed this duty one last time.

In the early evening Mom began to struggle even more to breathe and I requested more morphine. Her skin began to mottle and her hands and feet were even bluer. Still, I was not convinced she would pass that day and I prepared myself to spend the night by her in a chair that converted to a small bed. I spent much of my time talking with Mom and holding her hand. Paul sat in a chair behind me. My daughter Catlin arrived by 7 p.m. to say her good-bye. She always found it difficult to see her grandmother as a person with dementia and I admired her courage for showing up. As Catlin left, Mom visibly began to breathe much easier. Even the nurse noticed this. I turned on the TV for a break to watch some of *Glee* while I kept one eye focused on Mom. She looked like a fish out of water; her mouth formed an O as she very slowly breathed in and out.

After a short period I realized she was taking fewer breathes. I turned off the TV and in that instant both Paul and I recognized this was the end. I took Mom's hand as she made a strange gurgling noise. One more breath and that was it. She was still. The room suddenly echoed with her roaring oxygen machine. It was no longer needed and I shut it off, grateful to hear the silence.

The nurse came in. Paul and I both turned and said, "She is gone."

Her eyes grew wide and she pulled her stethoscope from her neck to listen.

"Yes," she concluded.

It was nine-fourteen p.m. The nurse called her supervisor to confirm her determination.

I sat with Mom and noticed her hands. I sobbed. Eventually, Paul and I stepped out of the room and the staff rushed in to clean her up and lay her flat before rigor mortis set in. They were also concerned about the oxygen tubes across her face; they didn't want them to leave a mark. The mask was removed; no longer of use.

Thankfully, all of the legal work Rocky and I had prepared was put into motion. Everything was already taken care of; there were no decisions to be made. The nurse called the funeral home. I kissed Mom one last time on her forehead. The gurney was brought in. I stood outside the door and only half watched as her body was covered. The staff cried as they helped remove Mom's body from her room and into the waiting hearse.

With that, Mom was gone.

Mom just a few days before her death
February 2012

## Home Again, Home Again, Jiggety Jig Jig

That little phrase, originally a Mother Goose rhyme, ran through my head as I pictured Mom in her casket being loaded onto a plane for her return home. Mom often said the jingle as she pulled the car into the garage after a long drive. I have heard myself doing the same over the years. It was late in the evening a few days after Mom's death and her body was returning to Indiana for burial. She would precede her children, grandchildren, and assorted spouses to Wabash by a few days.

Rocky and I spent the week and a half between Mom's death and her funeral tying up loose ends. I ordered the flowers and made final decisions with the funeral home. Rocky occupied herself with arranging for Mom's Celebration of Life. Both of us went through periods of relief and grief, knowing the ordeal of watching our Mom slowly die was over and yet crying over the loss of our mother.

One evening we were well into our second, perhaps third glass of wine. It had been a busy day with both of us on the phone and computer, responding to questions from siblings, figuring out logistics and making the final plans. Paul had an idea.

"Why don't you two go out to Indiana early and head to Purdue for a couple of days? I'm sure if you check you might even be able to catch a basketball game."

Our eyes lit up and a thrill shivered between us. Before we let the wine wear off and change our minds, we hopped on the computer and booked our flights. We arranged to spend two nights on the campus staying at the Purdue Memorial Union Hotel.

"Fantastic idea," both Rocky and I shrieked.

I smiled to Paul, and Rocky and I saluted him with a toast. I pulled my cell phone from the table and began texting Kristen. I wanted to give her a heads up, *Guess who is coming for a visit? Get ready because your mom and crazy Aunt Rocky will be there in a few days.* To Kristen's credit, she responded happily and said she looked forward to us getting there.

Callous? Perhaps. But Rocky and I didn't think that way. For over ten years we had been a team helping our mother survive after Dad passed away. If anyone needed to blow off steam before the funeral, it was us. We were anticipating a major blow up among seven strong minded siblings - a Christle Crisis we always called them. Rocky and I needed a few days to escape before we jumped into the fray.

Kristen wasn't able to pick us up at the airport. No matter, Rocky and I hopped onto the shuttle that travels between the airport and the Purdue campus. We grabbed a McDonald's hamburger and inhaled it with fries and a Coke as we stood in line with Purdue students heading back to campus. We all climbed aboard the small bus. Rocky and I managed to snag two seats across the aisle from each other. We settled in and watched as most of the students picked out their music, put in their earphones and pulled up their hoodies for the trip up Interstate sixty-five.

As we drove along, Rocky dozed off. I couldn't sleep. I kept thinking this would be one of the last times I set foot in Indiana. Certainly, I did not have any reason to return to Wabash after Mom's funeral. I reflected on my childhood and how this state had formed my early life and helped me develop into the woman I am today. I left in a hurry upon graduation from Purdue; I was ready to move far from my old life. I have never regretted that decision and now love my adopted home in upstate New York. One can never forget their roots, though, and I felt gratitude and sadness to realize this chapter of my life was now completely closed.

At last, our shuttle stopped in front of the Purdue Memorial Union. This hotel would be our home for the next two days. As we once again walked the cherished sidewalks of our Alma Mater, it was a trip down memory lane for these two Christle sisters. Purdue University brought back so many fantastic memories for both of us from our carefree youth: crisp football weekends, Indiana basketball fever and too many nights dancing and drinking.

We unpacked our bags as we waited for Kristen. Our first stop would be Harry's Chocolate Shoppe, the oldest bar in the area. It is just a few steps off the dry Purdue campus. Harry's hadn't changed much over the years and I swear they still had the same soundtrack from when I was on campus in the late 1970s. It is a favorite haunt of both students and alumni. Our party included just that; two alumni and one student. It was good to forget about our true visit to Indiana and kick back and enjoy ourselves. Professional therapy wouldn't have been nearly as beneficial.

The next evening was the highlight of our visit. I had purchased tickets online to the basketball game and, to our delight; we discovered the game was also senior night. This would be the last home game for the senior players.

As Rocky and I walked into the arena, searching for our seats we found ourselves amazed by the fact that we kept getting closer and closer to the floor. Much to our surprise, we finally landed five rows from the parquet and directly behind where our team huddled for time-outs.

As the game whistle was blown, Rocky and I high fived each other.

"Damn, girl, you did great finding these seats," Rocky yelled over the noise of the roaring crowd.

"I can't believe this. I can almost hear Coach Painter telling the boys what to do. It is so amazing to be this close and see what happens during timeouts. At home, the TV always breaks for a commercial."

Rocky and I yelled and rooted on the Boilermakers along with the students and other fans. We lost ourselves in the enthusiasm of the crowd. As we left the arena after the game, our excitement did not wane. Our feet took us on a familiar path across campus back to Harry's. Rocky could not let go of the wonderful feeling of the night and repeated several times, "I can't believe you and I are finally here at Purdue together. After so many years of telling ourselves we would do this. Here we are."

I just put my arm around her shoulders and gave her a big hug. I didn't want to reveal I was crying with gratitude for this glorious night.

The next day the mood was drastically different. Kristen pulled up to the Purdue Memorial Union in her decade old Jetta. Rocky and I solemnly piled in. It was definitely a college student's car. There was a lot of disrepair and junk everywhere. No matter, the little pile of bolts still had a lot of get up and go and transported us across Highway 24 into Wabash for our final tribute to Ruthanna "Corki" Christle.

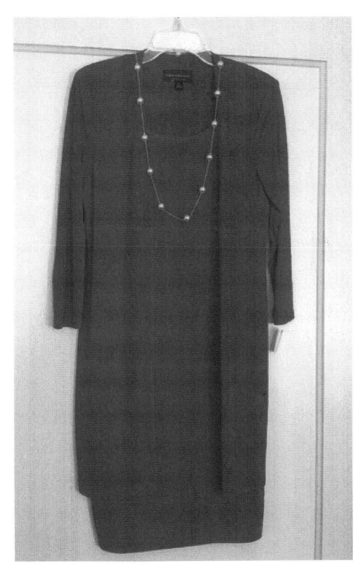

Mom's burial outfit

Rocky and me at the Purdue basketball game
February 2012

## Funeral

As I drove the once familiar roads between Purdue University and Wabash, I reflected on the planning Rocky and I had done months earlier. I was thankful that during this time of grieving, my siblings and I were not bogged down with arranging the funeral.

I thought back to the day in March 2010 when I flew to Atlanta. Feeling that Mom's life was drawing to an end, Rocky and I decided to get together and plan Mom's funeral and Celebration of Life service. We dedicated a week to our preparations.

There were many issues to consider. Mom converted to Catholicism as a young college girl, but after her children left the house Mom gradually attended Mass less often. After Dad died she stopped going all together. Rocky and I felt that while a Catholic burial was important to Dad, the same could not be said of Mom. We also considered the idea that the funeral was really for her children, none of whom still practiced that faith. It was decided, along with input from other siblings, that a Celebration of Life was more to our liking. Our thoughts stemmed from the fact that we mourned Mom and her ongoing death for years. A remembrance of the mother and woman Mom had once been was more fitting. Yet, a dilemma remained which was brought to our attention by Ranelle. Our oldest sibling felt some sort of religious ceremony should take place so a compromise was born: Instead of a funeral mass we had a candle lighting ceremony for family and close friends at the funeral home. The service took place before the burial.

A priest began and ended the program with prayers. The rest of the service included the following readings and tributes.

Ranelle read:

*From Ecclesiastes 3:1-8:*

*There is an appointed time for everything, and a time for every affair under the heavens.*

*A time to be born, and a time to die; a time to plant, and a time to uproot the plant.*

*A time to kill, and a time to heal: a time to tear down, and a time to build up.*

*A time to weep, and a time to laugh: a time to mourn, and a time to dance.*

*A time to scatter stones, and a time to gather them; a time to embrace, and a time to be far from embraces.*

*A time to seek, and a time to lose; a time to keep, and a time to cast away.*

*A time to rend, and a time to sew; a time to be silent, and a time to speak.*

*A time to love, and a time to hate; a time of war, and a time of peace.*

I read Mom's favorite prayer:

*The Prayer of St. Francis.*

*Lord, make me an instrument of Your peace. Where there is hatred, let me bring*

*love; Where there is injury, pardon; where*
*there is doubt, faith; where there is despair,*
*hope; where there is darkness, light; where*
*there is sadness, joy.*

*O Divine Master, grant that I may not so*
*much seek to be consoled as to console; to*
*be understood as to understand; to be loved*
*as to love. For it is in giving that we receive;*
*it is in pardoning that we are pardoned; it is*
*in dying that we are born to eternal life.*

During the ceremony one tall candle burned, representing Mom. Her children each lit a smaller candle from the tall one and passed the light on to their children. As the candles were lit from Mom's candle, through her children, then to her grandchildren and great-grandchildren, and onto friends, Rocky explained the symbolism.

*This one individual candle represents the*
*love of Ruthanna Christle, a light that still*
*burns even with her death. As a symbol of*
*her relationship with you, we ask each of*
*you to light your candle so that her one*

*candle will become many and her memories*
*can continue to live on in your heart.*

Once the candles were lighted, Rocky continued with a passage from "Tuesdays With Morrie" by Mitch Albom:

*As long as we can love each other, and*
*remember the feeling of love we had, we*
*can die without ever really going away. All*
*the love created is still there. All the*
*memories are still there. You live on-in the*
*hearts of everyone you touched and*
*nurtured while you were here. Death ends a*
*life, not a relationship.*

Rocky and I were pleased with the results of the ceremony we had created. We liked how we chose to honor our mother and the way it eased our family into the dreaded task of the burial service in the mind numbing cold of a windy Indiana February.

During our week of planning, Rocky and I felt there should be an additional tribute to the life our mother led. She touched so many people in Wabash as a teacher, counselor, judge, friend, bridge player and book club member. Rocky and I, along with encouragement from Rhonda, felt that a celebration of such a wonderful life would be appropriate.

Many days were spent brainstorming about what a celebration of life meant to us. Finally it was decided we would hold a public ceremony in the Honeywell Center in downtown Wabash. Appetizers were served along with coffee, tea, wine and beer. Most importantly so was dessert, as this was Mom's favorite food. Tables were set up; centerpieces, which Rocky made, were candles illuminating photos of Mom and her life. The tablecloths were red, Mom's favorite color. Her oldest grandson, Michael, was the emcee and each child and grandchild had the opportunity to speak or display any form of memory they wanted of their mother and grandmother.

Rocky designed an ad for the local newspaper. It invited the public to join in our celebration and politely requested that they also bring their own stories and pictures to share. We imagined a room filled with people whom Mom had touched with her life; sharing stories, laughter and, yes, even tears. Our hope was that we would send Mom off with joy and enthusiasm, the way she once led her life. Unsure of ourselves, we didn't know if the room would fill after all since so many friends had already passed and many of her students had moved away.

It was difficult for me to decide what I should say during the ceremony.  Since I was her caretaker in the final years, I decided I should speak about that.

I read the following:

> Forgive me if I don't appear grief-stricken. But with Mom's passing, I am beginning to see light as I emerge from my years of sadness as her caretaker. You see, the woman you all grieve for today, I have been grieving for years, as I watched her slip into dementia.
>
> I know my siblings will probably talk of memories of when we were young. I love those and have many. But, I thought I

would tell you briefly about Mom after she left her beloved Wabash.

After Dad died, Mom began calling me and my siblings for help with small issues. Many times her children would arrive to take care of her home and to visit.  One spring the calls became more frequent and when I arrived to help her, I realized she could no longer live alone. And that, simply, is why she moved to upstate New York with me and lived with my family.

Typical of Corki, she became a pal to my friends. She watched football with a Notre Dame alumnus. Cheering and reminiscing Mom loved telling friends that Dad would take down his beloved ND flag from the pole positioned in the front yard when he was disappointed with his team. Sometimes, she laughed, he would do this even in the middle of a game.

Mom played board and card games and talked about high school drama with my daughter Kristen. She discussed with Catlin her struggles and good times at Purdue. She laughed with my friends and me and, in her manner, helped us realize our concerns over children were just a dilemma, for now. There was much more to come in our lives and we shouldn't get caught up in the small conflicts of the moment.

Mom struggled with losing her mind. She knew what was going on and at times became frightened. It was difficult to stand by and not be able to console her or change the outcome. The best I could do was to provide a safe, clean, home, one she felt comfortable living in. When care was no longer possible at my home, Rocky and I searched out the perfect assisted living community for Mom.

We found Mom a beautiful home, with a view out her window of a bank of trees that mesmerized her with each season. One where she could see the moon and be comforted that Rhonda, her Moon buddy, was near. A home where she had her own space to live, with aides to watch over her and help, when needed.

Mom soon, as she had all her life, found those in need and became their champion. She held hands when fellow residents wanted comfort and warned the staff when others needed help. And, as in her whole life, with all people, the staff loved her. Many times when I would visit, I would find Mom having coffee with the staff in the kitchen. Mom also continued her independence. Once, when we could not find her, we located her in the opposite end of the residence sipping coffee. When asked what she was doing she replied, "the coffee is better over here."

When it became too difficult for Mom to continue at her assisted living community, Rocky and I again found a new community. Here was the help and additional nursing Mom needed, in a home with dignity. Consisting of small ranch style houses with private bedrooms, each had a huge kitchen table for the staff and residents to enjoy meals together and a living room for companionship.  She once again charmed the staff and her fellow residents. They held events and even cocktail parties on the patio, and we threw a family BBQ for her birthday. Always the helper of those in need, Mom insisted upon sitting next to her new woman friend, who did not talk, but loved to hold hands.

Mom left this life very gradually. I said good-bye every time I visited her. I said good-bye when she could no longer hold a conversation with me, or read her beloved books. I said good-bye when she lost the ability to discuss politics, when she could no longer walk on her own or smile and laugh about funny things her grandchildren were doing.

So today, I grieve my mother, but I also celebrate that she is once again in Joe's arms and playing a wicked game of bridge.

I struggled to read what I had written. I had to stop more than once to regain my composure. I wanted to tell her remaining friends and family left behind in Wabash, who so often worried about her, that Mom had ended her life as she had lived it: with compassion for others.

Dementia takes away one's dignity and leaves a dying shell in-between life and death. Rocky and I wanted to give Mom back her dignity and send her off with style.

I think we accomplished that.

Rhonda and Michael

Paul, Kristen, me, Catlin

Rocky

Rocky and me

I would like to acknowledge the following people for their support in creating this book, my writing teacher, Robyn Ringler and Writing Women's Minds: Sharon Spies, Maggie McDonald and Debbi Sabin for their ideas, first edits and encouragement. Special thanks to Debbi Sabin for the initial, time-consuming edit. I would also like to thank Laurie Carpenter for meeting with me and going over every sentence for grammar, content and flow as we worked through another edit of the book. In addition, Fran Yablonsky for her edits and comments. Finally, I want to send a special thank you to my friends and family who encouraged me in many varied ways, to continue with my dream of writing and to finish this book.

Made in the USA
Middletown, DE
22 December 2014